Framework FOCUS

D0505073

ICT

Dictionary

11-14

Steve Neal

Published by Letts Educational
The Chiswick Centre
414 Chiswick High Road
London W4 5TF
tel: 020 89963333
fax: 020 87428390
e-mail: mail@lettsed.co.uk
website: www.letts-education.com

Letts Educational Limited is a division of Granada Learning Limited, part of the Granada Media Group.

British Library Cataloguing in Publication Data

A catalogue record for this book is available from the British Library.

Acknowledgements
We are grateful to the following for permission to reproduce photographs: Apple Macintosh www.apple.com/uk/pr, pages 14 right, 45 right, 50 right, 71 right, 74 left; Art Directors & TRIP/Helene Rogers, pages 12 bottom left, 85 bottom left; Bite.pr.com, page 92; Corbis, pages 3 left, 52 left, 57 right; Education Photos/John Walmsley, page 62 bottom right; GeoScience Features, page 19 right; Getty Images/Benjamin Shearn, page 70 right; pages 3, 4 top right, 21 top left, 21 right, 22 top right, 22 bottom right, 26 left, 27 top right, 31 right, 37 left, 37 right, 41, 44 left, 49 right, 50 left, 60 top right, 71 left, 75 left, 78 left, 84 bottom right; Science Photo Library, pages 4 bottom left (Hank Morgan), 8 bottom right, 15 top left (Joseph Nettis), 67 left (Maximilian Stock Ltd, 73 left (Volker Steger/Siemens); Sony (UK) Ltd, pages 11 bottom right, 12 left, 58 left, 63 left, 80 right; Mark Wagner/aviation-images.com, page 22 left.

Cover photograph: Hugh Turvey/Science Photo Library

The author and publishers are grateful to the following for permission to reproduce copyright material.

Adobe®: Acrobat® Reader® p 24; Illustrator® p 35; ImageReady® p 36; Photoshop® p 43.

Apple Computer Inc: Mac OS® pp 1, 68, 88; Appleworks p 19. Mac OS and Appleworks are a trademark of Apple Computer, Inc., registered in the U.S. and other countries.

Freeserve: p 42.

Google Inc. pp 2, 30, 33, 72.

Microsoft Excel® pp iv, 1, 12, 14, 19, 66, 69, 76; Microsoft Internet Explorer® pp 2, 15, 30, 33, 59, 72, 82, 87; Microsoft Outlook Express® p 52; Microsoft PowerPoint® pp 2, 61, 62, 66, 74; Microsoft WindowsXP® p 21, 30, 54, 62; and Microsoft Word® pp 4, 8, 10, 16, 18, 25, 26, 31, 33, 36, 37, 40, 42, 55, 56, 57, 65, 72, 75, 79, 82, are registered trademarks of Microsoft Corporation. Screen shots reprinted by permission from Microsoft Corporation.

Jenni Morris p 3.

Netscape browser window© 2002 Netscape Communications Corporation. pp 8, 27, 28. Used with permission. Netscape Communications has not authorised, sponsored, endorsed, or approved this publication and is not responsible for its content.

RealNetworks for the use of RealPlayer® pp 9, 85. RealPlayer® is a registered trademark of RealNetworks, Inc.

VersionTracker.com p 59.

Illustrations: Ken Vail Graphic Design, Cambridge

Commissioned by Helen Clark

Project management by Vicky Butt

Editing by Jean Rustean

Design by Ken Vail Graphic Design, Cambridge

Production by PDQ

Printed and bound by Canale, Italy

How to use this dictionary

The Letts ICT Dictionary is aimed at Key Stage 3 ICT students, although other students will also benefit from its clear explanations and interesting detail. Text and layout have been designed to make the dictionary easy to use, including many features to help you understand as much about the words as about the technological ideas. This will make you more confident when you meet the words in your reading, and when you use them in your writing. These features are described in the examples below.

Entry word, or headword
The main form of the word. Unusual forms of the word are given in brackets after the headword.

Symbol
Any symbol or abbreviation of the headword is given in square brackets.

Definition
The meaning of the word. This is kept as clear and concise as possible.

Example
An example of the headword being used in a sentence.

Related words
Other entries in the dictionary related to the headword.

at [@]   ✉

preposition

@ is a symbol for 'at' and is used in an email address before the domain name. The convention is for the person's name or user identity to be followed by @ and then the domain name.

eg Jake Bond works for Sloopydog and his email address is Jake.Bond@sloopydog.co.uk

➡ **domain name**

Topic area
The area in ICT in which the word is most commonly used (see full list on the next page).

Part of speech
This tells you the job that the word does in a sentence.

Other meanings
If a word has more than one meaning, each meaning is numbered and each is followed by its own example.

synthesise

(*sin-the-size*)

verb

1 To synthesise is to bring together separate elements or things.

eg In music recording you use a synthesiser to synthesise different sounds.

2 To synthesise is to combine various factors so as to form a new, complex product/scenario.

eg The variables in the model were used to synthesise possible outcomes for profit from the concert.

Pronunciation
How to say the word.

Illustration
Visual examples rather than verbal examples are given where appropriate.

Information
Background information on the word and its use.

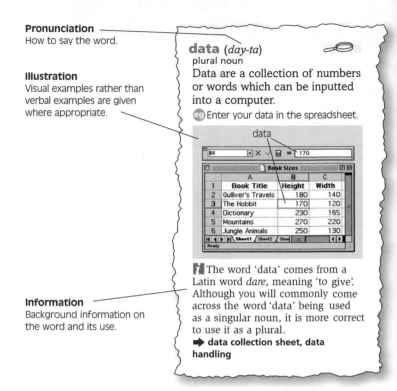

data (*day-ta*)
plural noun

Data are a collection of numbers or words which can be inputted into a computer.

🔵 Enter your data in the spreadsheet.

data

🛈 The word 'data' comes from a Latin word *dare*, meaning 'to give'. Although you will commonly come across the word 'data' being used as a singular noun, it is more correct to use it as a plural.

➡ **data collection sheet, data handling**

Topic areas

Each entry is labelled with an icon which tells you its topic area:

- ✍ Developing ideas
- 🔍 Finding things out
- ✉ Exchanging and sharing information
- 🔄 Reviewing, modifying and evaluating

Aa *Aa* Aa Яӑ **Aa**

absolute cell reference [$]
noun

When a spreadsheet formula is entered into a cell, it often refers to another cell. If the formula is copied, it adjusts to its new location. If you do not want it to adjust, but always need it to point to the same cell, you can use absolute cell referencing. This is usually done by putting dollar signs in front of the row and column coordinates. A2 is a cell reference, A2 is an absolute cell reference and will not change when copied.

🔵 The VAT rate is stored in one cell and needs to be used in calculations throughout the spreadsheet, so it is addressed by absolute cell referencing.

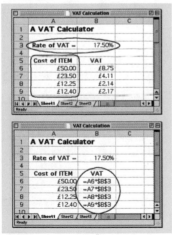

➡ cell, relative cell referencing, spreadsheet

accuracy (*ak-yur-a-see*)
noun

The accuracy of something is how correct it is.

🔵 Melanie checked the accuracy of the clock on her computer.

accurate
adjective

If something is accurate then it is correct or faithful to an original.

🔵 Roxy checked that the data was accurate before she entered it into her bar chart.

acknowledgement
(*ak-no-lij-ment*)
noun

An acknowledgement is a recognition that you have used something produced by someone else.

🔵 In the acknowledgments at the end of her essay, Jill listed all the websites she had used.
➡ attribute

adapt
verb

To adapt means to modify or to adjust something.

🔵 He was able to adapt the template so that it was suitable for the newsletter.

A B C D E F G H I J K L M N O P Q R S T U V W X Y Z

A

B C D E F G H I J K L M N O P Q R S T U V W X Y Z

address
noun

In a spreadsheet, the address is the name given to a particular cell. Each column has a letter of the alphabet and each row has a number, so the address A1 would be column A, row 1.

eg 'Make a note of the address of your Total cost cell', said Mr. Matthews.

address book
noun ✉

An address book, or address list, is a feature in e-mail programs such as Outlook Express. E-mail addresses and other contact details can be added to it.

eg Neil added Sam's e-mail address and phone number to the address book on his computer.

analogue (*a-na-log*)
adjective

An analogue signal is one which can take any value between the lowest and the highest. Analogue values are not used by computers. They use digital signals which are either on or off.

eg The modem converts the computer's digital signals to the analogue signals needed on the local telephone system.

➡ **digital**

AND
noun 🔍

AND is one of the Boolean connectors used in computing, and is one of the advanced search options on some search engines. By typing 'AND' you can refine your search to include additional words.

eg If you select all where the last name = Smith then AND where first name = John and you will find all records with the name 'John Smith'.

➡ **Boolean connector, NOT, OR**

animate
verb (noun: animation) ✉

To animate something means to bring it to life. A series of still images can be animated so that they appear to move.

eg An animation was added to the PowerPoint presentation.

annotate
verb 🔗

To annotate is to add notes or comments to a piece of writing.

eg The teacher decided to annotate Bob's essay to show Bob where he had made mistakes.

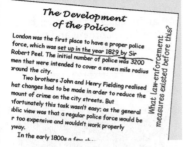

The Development of the Police

London was the first place to have a proper police force, which was set up in the year 1829 by Sir Robert Peel. The initial number of police was 3200 men that were intended to cover a seven mile radius around the city.

Two brothers John and Henry Fielding realised that changes had to be made in order to reduce the amount of crime on the city streets. But unfortunately this task wasn't easy; as the general public view was that a regular police force would be far too expensive and wouldn't work properly anyway.

In the early 1800s a few ...

What law-enforcement measures existed before this?

appraise (a-prayz)
verb

To appraise is to judge the worth of something.

 The group decided to appraise their presentation before they delivered it.

archive (ar-kiyv)
verb

To archive data means to put it into store in case it is needed in the future. The original copy is then deleted.

eg The details of all the items that were sold this year were archived to make more room on the hard disk for this year's figures.

archives
noun

Archives are stores of data that are not used very often but may occasionally be required in the future.

eg The exam results of the students who left this year were deleted from the management system files and placed in the school's archives.

assess
verb

To assess is to judge or evaluate.

eg Rupert had to assess whether the website was suitable for his purpose.

assessment
noun

An assessment is a judgement or an evaluation of something.

eg The girls carried out an assessment of their presentation to check that it met the brief.

assumption (a-sump-shun)
noun

An assumption is something that is taken for granted or believed.

eg His assumption was that the information on the CD-ROM was correct.

at [@]
preposition

@ is a symbol for 'at' and is used in an e-mail address before the domain name. The convention is for the person's name or user identity to be followed by @ and then the domain name.

eg Jake Bond works for Sloopydog and his e-mail address is Jake.Bond@sloopydog.co.uk

➡ domain name

A
B
C
D
E
F
G
H
I
J
K
L
M
N
O
P
Q
R
S
T
U
V
W
X
Y
Z

atmosphere (*at-mos-feer*)
noun

The atmosphere is the mixture of gases that surround the Earth.

eg Weather satellites take 'pictures' of the Earth's atmosphere. Sensors on the satellite measure energy waves that radiate and reflect from the Earth's atmosphere below. The data is then sent by radio to powerful computers on Earth.

➡ sensor

attribute
1 verb (*a-tri-byoot*)

To attribute is to acknowledge or give credit for something.

eg The class were told it was essential to attribute the sources they had used in their reports.

2 noun (*a-tri-byoot*)

An attribute is a feature of something

eg The children had to make a list of the different attributes of chocolate bars such as the wrapper, cost or make.

audience (*or-dee-ents*)
noun

The audience are a group of people who watch or view something.

Audience can also be used to refer to the intended readers of a piece of writing.

eg The audience for the live broadcast was a group of Year 7 students.

audio cassette recorder
noun

An audio cassette recorder is a device for recording and playing back sound on a cassette tape.

eg The teacher recorded the discussion on an audio cassette recorder.

audit trail
noun

An audit trail is a record of the transactions carried out on a computer system.

eg The programmer examined the audit trail to see if he could identify the reported error.

authentic (*or-then-tik*)
adjective

Authentic means genuine.

eg A computer can check whether a user is authentic by asking for a password.

➡ authenticity, password

authenticity (*or-then-ti-si-ty*)
noun

Authenticity is when something has the quality of being authentic. It is used in information technology with regard to users of computers or websites.

eg The authenticity of users attempting to open the file was checked by means of a password.

➡ authentic, e-commerce, password

automate

verb

To automate is to use computers to control equipment or perform routines/self-regulate without the need for direct human intervention or supervision.

🔵 The system was fully automated which meant the company saved money on staffing costs.

➡ robot

automated process
noun

An automated process is where the stages of an operation or process are carried out without the need for human intervention. Specific software can be designed to carry out an automated process.

🔵 The pharmaceutical industry will use an automated process to manufacture a new drug in order to make the process more efficient, accurate and consistent.

automatic
adjective

An event is automatic if it does not require a human to make a decision.

🔵 The automatic door does not need to be pushed, it will open by itself when someone approaches.

average (*a-va-rij*)
noun

An average is a number which represents the normal or middle value in a set of data.

🔵 Her average income for the last three years was £25,000.

A
B
C
D
E
F
G
H
I
J
K
L
M
N
O
P
Q
R
S
T
U
V
W
X
Y
Z

Bb

backup
noun

A backup is a copy of a file. It is made in case the original is lost or damaged. A backup can be made on the hard drive of a computer, a tape, a CD-RW, a floppy disc, a zip drive, or on a server.

eg Mr. Matthews regularly reminded his pupils to make backup copies of important files.

➡ **CD-RW, floppy disc, server, storage, tapes, zip drive**

band width
noun

Band width is a measurement of the speed at which a signal is transmitted between computers and servers. The unit of band width is bits per second.

eg The available band width determines how quickly websites download to your computer and whether you are able to access video.

➡ **bit, broadband, Internet service provider (ISP)**

bar chart
noun

A bar chart is a chart that uses bars of equal width to represent statistics. This may appear horizontally.

eg Frank used a bar chart to show the pupils' favourite sports.

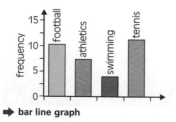

➡ **bar line graph**

bar code
noun

The vertical black stripes of different widths printed on the packaging of products is the bar code. Encoded in the stripes is a number which identifies the product and its price. It is also linked to automatic stock reordering.

eg The bar code on the book automatically told the stock-control system to generate an order for another copy from the supplier.

and

➡ **EAN, EFTPOS**

bar line graph
noun

A bar line graph is a bar chart where the bars appear as lines. This may appear horizontally.

eg A bar line graph was used to show the traffic flow outside the school.

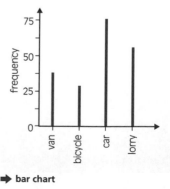

➡ **bar chart**

6

bespoke software
noun

Bespoke software has been especially written for a user or client, rather than purchased off the shelf. It is made to measure to the user's needs.

🔵 The travel agent commissioned some bespoke software for keeping records and communicating with customers.

beta release (bee-ta) 🔗
noun

A beta release is a prototype of a piece of software, released for testing, so that bugs can be eliminated.

🔵 Steve downloaded the beta release of the new browser so that he could test it on his own machine.

🔳 Beta is the second letter of the Greek alphabet. It comes after the first letter called alpha. You can have an alpha release of software that comes before the beta release.

bias
noun

Bias is a one-sided view or influence that does not present the full picture.

🔵 The teacher asked the pupils to find evidence of bias in the article on the website.

bit
noun

A bit is the basic unit of information in computing. A bit is a binary digit with a value of either 0 or 1.

🔵 The website took a while to download because of the number of bits in each of the images.

➡ **bitmap, bitmapped graphic**

bitmap
noun
A bitmap is a way that a

computer can store the details of a picture as a series of dots. It usually takes up a lot of storage space.

🔵 Na embedded a picture of herself in the letter that she word processed and sent to her parents in China. It made the file very large because it was a bitmap and took a long time to download.

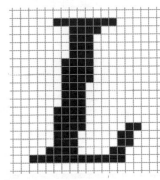

➡ **vector graphics**

bitmapped graphic
noun

A bitmapped graphic is a picture which has been processed as a set of dots. Each dot is stored separately on the computer system.

🔵 Helen produced a graph showing projected sales and embedded it in her presentation as a bitmapped graphic.

➡ **vector graphics**

body text ✉
noun

The body text is the main part of a document rather than the header and footer.

🔵 The body text was hidden as Jenny added a header and footer to the document.

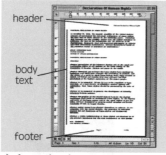

header

body text

footer

➡ footer, header

bold ✉
adjective

Bold text has heavy, dark lines so that it stands out. The option to make text bold appears on the toolbar of word-processing or DTP software.

🔵 Kauser used bold text for the title of her newsletter so that it made a greater impact.

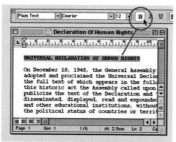

➡ desktop publishing (DTP), formatting, text

bookmark 🔍
1 noun

A bookmark is the name for a website saved for future reference on the browser, Netscape

Navigator. This is similar to the Favourites option on Internet Explorer.

2 verb

To bookmark a site is to save it for future reference.

🔵 The pupils were told to bookmark any suitable sites they found so that later they could find them easily.

➡ web browser

Boole 🔍
noun

George Boole was a nineteenth-century English mathematician who invented a system of symbolic logic on which modern computing is based. The symbolic logic is used in the construction of processors, programming and searches of databases. It has two values: true and false, represented by 0 and 1.

🔵 The symbolic logic invented by George Boole had a significant influence on the development of present day computers.

➡ AND, Boolean connector, NOT, OR

Boolean connector
noun

The Boolean connectors include AND, OR and NOT. They can be used to conduct searches of databases, and are the basis of advanced search engines on the Internet.

eg Boolean connectors allow you to search for combinations of words or phrases.

➡ AND, Boole, NOT, OR

bounce
verb ✉

E-mails are said to bounce when they return to the sender because the address of the person to whom it was sent could not be found.

eg The e-mail was bounced back to Jill as undeliverable, so she checked to see if she had entered the correct address.

broadband
noun ✉

Broadband is a communications medium that can carry a wide range of frequencies including video. As well as providing a faster Internet connection it is also used for telephones and cable television.

eg Broadband means that you can talk on the phone while watching videos on your computer.

➡ band width, ISDN

browse
verb

To browse means to search for or look through something in a leisurely way. It has come to mean the action of searching the Internet.

eg For her Geography homework Ali decided to browse the web for information on earthquakes.

➡ Internet, search engine, surf, web browser

browser
➡ web browser

buffering
noun ✉

Buffering is the process whereby fluctuating data from any peripheral is temporarily stored before being accessed by the receiving program. The buffering message is often seen in software when downloading audio and video clips.

eg Eddy had to wait for the buffering to be completed before he could play the sample album track he had downloaded.

➡ MP3

bug
noun ✉

A bug is an error in a computer program. Before software is released it is tested for bugs – this is called debugging.

eg If you have problems with a piece of software it may have a bug, so you will need to get a patch.

➡ patch

A

B

C

D

E

F

G

H

I

J

K

L

M

N

O

P

Q

R

S

T

U

V

W

X

Y

Z

bullet points ✉
noun (singular: bullet point)

The option to insert bullet points appears on the toolbar of word-processing or DTP software. Bullet points are a series of large dots and can be used for the formatting of text, usually when the writer wants to list a series of points.

eg Bullet points were used in the leaflet to list the dangers of smoking.

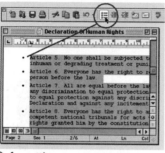

➡ **formatting**

burn ✉
verb

To burn is to create a CD by copying data onto a CD-RW or CD-R disk.

eg John decided to burn a copy of the new mix he had created.

➡ **CD-R, CD-RW**

byte ✉
noun

A byte is usually a set of eight binary digits which can be treated as a single unit.

eg A byte is the smallest unit of storage.

i Like all computer vocabulary, byte is a relatively new word. It was created in the 20th century as a combination of 'bit' and bite'.

➡ **bit**

cache (*kash*)
noun

The cache is an area of fast memory in a computer that temporarily stores web pages you have visited. Because they are stored your browser can access them more quickly.

eg If you use 'Back' on the browser Internet Explorer, the web page you then see will be accessed from the cache on your computer.

➡ web browser

CAD
➡ computer-aided design

calculate
verb

To calculate is to produce an answer to a numerical problem by using mathematical techniques.

eg Vicky needed to calculate the total profit from all of this month's sales.

calculation
noun

A calculation is the process by which a numerical problem is solved by mathematics.

eg The calculation showed that the company would lose money this month.

CAM
➡ computer-aided manufacturing

capital letters
noun (singular: capital letter)

The large letters used at the start of a sentence or for a proper noun are capital letters.

eg Capital letters are called upper case letters in word-processing software.

➡ lower case, upper case

capture
verb

To capture is to collect data in a form that is suitable for computer processing.

eg The customer filled in an order form. This form captured the data needed to make up the order.

CD-R
noun/abbreviation

CD-R stands for Compact Disk Recordable. A CD-R can be used only once to record or store data such as a copy of a CD containing music.

eg John recorded a copy of the music he had composed for his friends on to a CD-R.

➡ CD-ROM, CD-RW, CD-RW drive, DVD, storage

CD-ROM
➡ Compact disk read-only memory

Sidebar letters: A B C D E F G H I J K L M N O P Q R S T U V W X Y Z

CD-RW
noun/abbreviation

CD-RW stands for Compact Disk ReWriteable. A CD-RW is similar to a CD-R but it can be used many times over; the data can be erased and new data added each time it is used.

eg A CD-RW is an excellent way of storing copies of important files.

➡ **CD-ROM, CD-R, CD-RW drive, DVD**

CD-RW drive
noun/abbreviation

A CD-RW drive stands for Compact Disk Read Write drive. The drive can be external or built into a computer, and it allows the user to copy CDs or to copy files to it.

eg A CD-RW drive is essential if you want to make copies of CDs.

➡ **burn, CD-R, CD-ROM, DVD**

cell (*sell*)
noun

A cell is a space in a spreadsheet grid where data or a formula can be displayed. It is also used to refer to a space in the gridlines of a table in a word-processing package.

eg Information on the height and width of various books was entered in the cells in the spreadsheet.

cell

	A	B	C
1	Book Title	Height	Width
2	Gulliver's Travels	180	140
3	The Hobbit	170	120
4	Dictionary	230	165
5	Mountains	270	220
6	Jungle Animals	250	130

cell reference
noun

A cell reference is the address of a cell in a spreadsheet grid. Each cell reference has two elements: a vertical coordinate and a horizontal coordinate. The columns in a spreadsheet are indicated by letters – A, B, C etc. The rows are indicated by numbers – 1, 2, 3, etc. So the address of a cell could be K4.

eg He moved the data from cell reference K23 to D4.

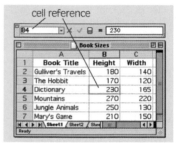

cell reference

	A	B	C
1	Book Title	Height	Width
2	Gulliver's Travels	180	140
3	The Hobbit	170	120
4	Dictionary	230	165
5	Mountains	270	220
6	Jungle Animals	250	130
7	Mary's Game	210	150

➡ **absolute cell reference, column, row**

census (*sen-sus*)
noun

A census is an official count of the population, including various details about each inhabitant. A census is carried out in the UK every 10 years.

eg The 1901 census should be available online.

chart
noun

A chart is a diagram representing numerical values.

eg He converted the information on the spreadsheet into a pie chart.

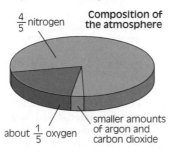

$\frac{4}{5}$ nitrogen

Composition of the atmosphere

about $\frac{1}{5}$ oxygen

smaller amounts of argon and carbon dioxide

➡ **bar chart, pie chart, spreadsheet**

check
verb

To check something is to look at it and ensure that everything is correct and as it should be.

eg It's always a good idea to check your answers before the end of an exam.

clarity
noun

The clarity of something is how clear it is.

eg Read over your essay and check for clarity.

class interval
noun

When collecting data, each class or group is bound by the limits of the class interval.

eg I grouped the ages of students in my survey into the following class intervals: 7 to 10, 11 to 13 and 14 to 16.

classify
verb

To classify information is to arrange it in classes or categories.

eg Roger had to decide how to classify the information he had found on the Internet.

click through
verb

When a website user clicks on a link to an advertiser's website from a web page they are said to 'click through'.

eg The advertiser will pay the owner of the original website a fee for a set number of users who 'click through'.
➡ **e-commerce**

clip art
noun

Clip art is a generic term for copyright-free images or photographs. These are readily available on CD-ROMs and websites. They can be used to enhance your work.

eg Matthew searched through the clip art to find a suitable image for his PowerPoint presentation.

colour scheme
noun

A colour scheme is a set of colours chosen for a publication or website and used consistently throughout.

eg Green and gold was the chosen colour scheme for the school website.

column (co-lum)

noun

A column is the space between two vertical lines that run down a spreadsheet or table.

eg It was decided to add another column in the spreadsheet to display the data.

column

	A	B	C
	Book Title	Height	Width
1			
2	Gulliver's Travels	180	140
3	The Hobbit	170	120
4	Dictionary	230	165
5	Mountains	270	220
6	Jungle Animals	250	130
7	Mary's Game	210	150
8	Famous People	260	200
9	Oliver Twist	170	120
10	The Tudors	280	200

➡ row, spreadsheet, table

compact disk read-only memory [CD-ROM]
noun

A compact disk with read-only memory, commonly known as a CD-ROM, can be read by a computer, but the information cannot be added to or altered. CD-ROMs are used for distributing software.

eg In order to install the new software, Vicky loaded the CD-ROM into the appropriate drive on her computer.

➡ CD-R, CD-RW, drive, digital video disk (DVD)

comparative
adjective

The word comparative is used to describe the action of comparing more than two methods or ways of doing something.

eg The teacher asked the class to examine the information from two websites for comparative purposes.

computer
noun

A computer is a machine that carries out calculations with numerical or other stored data. Originally computers could be mechanical or electronic, but the word computer is now usually just used for electronic machines.

ⅰ The first mechanical computer was designed by Charles Babbage in 1835. The first electronic computer was built by Thomas Flowers and Alan Turing in 1943.

eg The computer has completely altered the nature of the modern office.

➡ personal computer

computer-aided design [CAD]
noun

Computer-aided design, or CAD, is the use of computer software to design industrial products such as cars, washing machines etc. The 3-D models on computers allow the designer to explore alternative shapes and lines.

eg CAD is concerned with the drawing or physical layout steps of engineering design.

➡ CAM

computer-aided manufacturing [CAM]
noun

Computer-aided manufacturing, or CAM, is the use of computer software to carry out such tasks as controlling the machine tools in a factory or the ordering of components in a warehouse. CAD is often linked with CAM as the design and manufacturing processes are closely linked.

eg CAM is used to control the robots on car assembly lines.

➡ CAD

computer conferencing
noun ✉

Computer conferencing is the process of holding a discussion between people at different locations using the Internet. Users talk to each other by posting messages on forums.

eg Computer conferencing is a good medium for discussions when it's difficult to get people to meet face to face.

➡ forum, moderate, video conferencing

computer crime
noun ✉

A computer crime is an illegal activity involving a computer. Computer crimes include hacking into systems, illegally transferring money from bank accounts and stealing credit card details.

eg There are special police units in the UK for investigating computer crime.

➡ hacking

conclusion
noun

A conclusion is the judgement or decision you reach after examining the evidence.

eg Essays need to have a conclusion.

content
noun

The content is the words, music or images placed on a website. The content is distinct from the technical or design features of the site.

eg 'Content is king' is a slogan from the dotcom days of the Internet. It means that content is the most important thing on a website.

content

➡ contents list, dotcom

contents list
noun

A contents list is usually on the opening page of a website and gives details of what can be

A B **C** D E F G H I J K L M N O P Q R S T U V W X Y Z

A
B
C
D
E
F
G
H
I
J
K
L
M
N
O
P
Q
R
S
T
U
V
W
X
Y
Z

found on the other pages. It is sometimes called a table of contents.

🔵 David checked the Letts site to see if the contents list contained study advice.

Schools ordering copie will receive them at the

➡ content, dotcom

continuous data

(*con-ti-new-us day-ta*)
noun

Data which can take any value between the lowest and the highest possible is called continuous data.

🔵 The teacher measured the height of each child. All the measurements were different because it was continuous data.

control

noun

Control is a branch of ICT studies. It is when instructions are placed in a sequence to make something behave in a particular way. A desired action is broken down into a series of steps: work out the correct sequence, conduct a trial, analyse the results and carry out modifications.

🔵 To be good at control in Design and Technology you have to be good at systematic thinking.

➡ Logo

control loop

noun

A control loop is a series of

instructions that are repeated until a certain condition is met.

🔵 The control loop allowed the barrier to be raised until the car park was full.

➡ control

control technique

noun

Control technique is the way that a computer is used to operate another device such as a robot or buggy.

🔵 Jim set the computer to operate a set of traffic lights using control techniques.

cookie ✉

noun

A cookie is a small file placed on the hard drive of your computer by the server of a website you have visited. When you revisit the site the cookie identifies you and customised web pages can be provided.

🔵 You can customise your browser so that cookies are not automatically stored on your hard drive.

➡ web browser

copy ✉

verb

To copy means to duplicate. The instruction 'Copy' can be found under the 'Edit' menu in software and also in the tool bar as a symbol. Text and pictures can be copied and then pasted elsewhere.

🔵 Highlight the text you need before selecting Copy from the Edit menu.

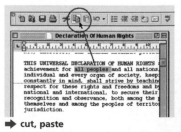

➡ cut, paste

copyright
noun

Copyright is the legal ownership of writing, images and music. For example, authors automatically have copyright on their work. If you want to quote from someone else's material in your school work, you should make an acknowledgements list – a list of your sources – at the end.

eg The material found on websites is often protected by copyright.

➡ **acknowledgement**

corporate image
noun ✉

The corporate image is how a company portrays itself to the public through such things as its stationery, website, logo or brochures.

eg The graphic design company provided a new corporate image for the company by developing a new logo and colour scheme for the brochures, exhibition stands and stationery.

➡ **logo**

correlation (co-re-lay-shun)
noun

Correlation means the connection between two variables. It can be found by drawing a scatter graph and seeing whether a clear pattern is visible.

eg There was found to be a correlation between shoe size and height.

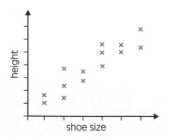

➡ **line of best fit, scatter graph**

counter
noun

A counter is a variable (part of computer storage) which can be used to record how many times something has happened. The expression 'hit counter' is also used to describe a website display that shows the number of visitors to the site.

eg Brodie wrote a procedure in Logo to draw ten triangles. She used a counter to control the number produced.

Visitors to this site this month

003588

➡ **variable**

criteria (cry-teer-ee-ya)
noun (singular: criterion)

Criteria are the standards against which something is judged.

eg The website was measured against the criteria of accessibility and readability.

critical audience
noun

A critical audience is an audience which reads a document or listens to a presentation and then offers an opinion on the quality.

eg The presentation at the interview took place before a critical audience.

criticise (cri-ti-size)
noun

To criticise is to pass judgement on something or to find fault.

eg The readers of the document felt the need to criticise it because of the poor layout.

A
B
C
D
E
F
G
H
I
J
K
L
M
N
O
P
Q
R
S
T
U
V
W
X
Y
Z

A
B
C
D
E
F
G
H
I
J
K
L
M
N
O
P
Q
R
S
T
U
V
W
X
Y
Z

crop
verb

To crop is to cut out the unwanted margin areas of a picture.

🔵 Jack decided to crop the picture in order to focus on the subject.

cumulative frequency
noun

Cumulative frequency is found by adding previous amounts to each group's frequency until the total frequency is found.

🔵 The data in a cumulative frequency table can also be displayed as a graph.

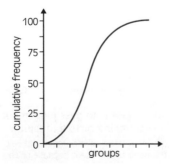

cursor
noun

The cursor is the mark that blinks on your computer screen at the place in the text where the next character will be inserted.

🔵 The cursor can either be moved by the mouse or the cursor keys.

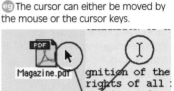

cursor

cut
verb

To cut means to remove. The instruction 'Cut' can be found under the 'Edit' menu in software and also on the toolbar as a symbol. Part of a document or picture can be cut and then pasted elsewhere.

🔵 To cut and paste effectively is a valuable skill when drafting essays.

➡ copy, paste

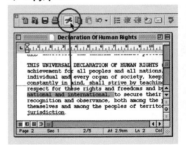

data (*day-ta*)
plural noun

Data are a collection of numbers or words which can be inputted into a computer.

eg Enter your data in the spreadsheet.

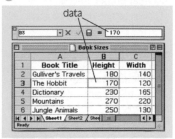

data

🔍 The word 'data' comes from a Latin word *dare*, meaning 'to give'. Although you will commonly come across the word 'data' being used as a singular noun, it is more correct to use it as a plural.

➡ **data collection sheet, data handling**

database
noun

A database is an organised way of storing information on a computer so that it can be found quickly.

eg The e-mail addresses of previous customers were kept on a database so that details of special offers could be sent to them.

data collection sheet
noun

A data collection sheet is used to record observed data.

eg The traffic flow was recorded on a data collection sheet.

➡ **data, data handling**

datalogger
noun

A datalogger is any device which automatically measures changes using electronic sensors, for example a speed camera. The data collected by the datalogger is transferred to a computer.

eg A datalogger can be used for measuring temperature changes within a lava flow.

➡ **datalogging**

datalogging
noun

Datalogging is the continuous transfer of data from a sensor to either a temporary storage device (a datalogger) or directly to a computer.

A B C **D** E F G H I J K L M N O P Q R S T U V W X Y Z

A B C D E F G H I J K L M N O P Q R S T U V W X Y Z

eg The pupils carried out a datalogging exercise involving the effect of temperature on plant growth.
➡ **remote datalogging**

data handling
noun

Data handling is the process of moving data around in a computer system and carrying out a variety of actions on the data.

eg A list of all the pupils who travelled to school by car was produced using data handling software.

Data Protection Act
noun 🔗

The Data Protection Act is a law that came into effect in the UK in 1998. It states how information about individual people should be gathered, stored, and distributed. For example, it states that a company has to ask your permission before passing on personal data about you.

eg It was Mr Bates's job to ensure that the school's website met the regulations specified in the Data Protection Act.

data retrieval
noun

Finding and extracting the right data from a database is known as data retrieval.

eg Nurse Powell found quick data retrieval essential when identifying the correct patients for her drug trial.

data structure
noun

A data structure is a way of organising data in a logical and consistent way. One data structure is to group the data about different things into different tables.

eg The data structure that the programmer set up for the video shop

was one table for video details, one table for customer details and another to hold details of videos out on hire.
➡ **table**

data type
noun

Programming and databases have to specify the data type they use. Common types include whole numbers (integers), numbers with decimal points, and text.

eg When setting up the database, John specified text as one of the data types.

delete (*de-leet*) [**Del**] ✉
verb

To delete is to remove.

eg 'Use the correct key to delete unnecessary words from your stories,' said the teacher.

design brief ✉
noun

The design brief is a document created by the client and given to those people who will be working on the design of the product. It is a guide for the designers. The design brief will give details of the client's objectives, how they need to work, what they need to get from the process and when they need to get it.

eg The design brief specified that the product had to appeal to young people and to be reasonably priced.

desktop computer
noun

A desktop computer has a separate monitor, keyboard and processing unit.

eg Desktop computers are not as portable as laptop computers.

➡ **laptop**

desktop publishing [DTP]
noun

Desktop publishing is a general name for a type of software. Desktop publishing allows the user to produce sophisticated documents using images, graphics and different layouts.

eg Eddy used the desktop publishing software to produce a professional-looking skateboarding magazine.

➡ **graphics**

develop
verb

To develop is to take something onto the next, more organised stage.

eg Janet was told to develop her project in greater detail.

dial up
verb

This is the action of a computer dialling a telephone number in order to make a connection between one computer and another.

eg Julie's computer dialled up her service provider's server.

digital (*di-jit-al*)
adjective

Data is described as digital if it can only be in one state or another. A digital data item is either true or false, 0 or 1, on or off. Computers use digital methods for storing and sending data. Digital equipment is more reliable than analogue equipment.

eg The scanner produced a digital version of the image so that the computer could store it.

➡ **analogue**

digital camera
noun

A digital camera captures images and stores them as digital files which can be transferred to a computer for editing and printing.

eg You can improve the quality of your pictures by using a digital camera and then editing them.

digital divide
noun

The digital divide is the gap in society between those who have access to the new technologies, such as computers and the Internet, and those who do not.

A B C D E F G H I J K L M N O P Q R S T U V W X Y Z

(eg) The digital divide means that more than 80% of people in the world have never even heard a dial tone, let alone surfed the Web.

digital video disk or digital versatile disk [DVD]

noun

A digital video disk, or DVD, is a read-only optical disk mainly used for home entertainment such as films. A DVD can be played through a dedicated machine or games player, but computers can also have a DVD drive. A DVD is similar to a CD-ROM but has a greater storage capacity.

(eg) The time on the aeroplane passed quickly as he watched a film on DVD on his laptop.

➡ CD-ROM, DVD-RW

digital video software
noun

Digital video software is used to edit moving images taken with a video camera. The images can be deleted or placed in a different order and sound and other effects can be added.

(eg) Emily used digital video software to edit her video of the school fete.

discrete data
noun

Separate or distinct items or groups of data are known as discrete data.

(eg) Shoe sizes are discrete data.

disk drive
noun

A disk drive is a storage device on a computer that reads and writes data.

(eg) John's new laptop had a floppy disk drive and a CD-RW disk drive.

➡ CD-ROM, CD-RW, DVD, floppy disk, hard disk drive, zip drive

display
noun

The display, sometimes called the screen or monitor, is the part of a computer where the user can see their work and the software controls.

(eg) She adjusted the controls on the display to make her work easier to see.

➡ monitor

distance–time graph
noun

A distance–time graph is a diagram showing how distance varies with time.

eg) The data on the spreadsheet was converted into a distance–time graph.

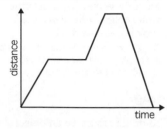

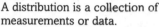

distribution
noun

A distribution is a collection of measurements or data.

eg) Rob collected all the information about dietary preferences. He then drew up a frequency table to show the distribution of his groups.

document
noun

A document is an electronic file that can consist of words, images or numbers. It is written in everyday language rather than in language used for programming computers.

eg) Frank e-mailed his geography homework to his teacher as an attached document.

document formatting
noun

Document formatting is the process of changing the appearance of a document rather than its content. This includes changing the font style and size, margins and indents.

eg) When document formatting, one of the most important things to consider is selecting a suitable font.
➡ font

documentation

noun

The user guides or manuals that accompany new software or hardware are known as the documentation.

eg) Andy took a look at the documentation for advice on how to network his computer system.

domain
noun

A domain is group of computers linked together on a network, with part of their address in common.

eg) John knew by the address that the computers belonged to the same domain.
➡ domain name

domain name
noun

A domain name can be given to a server or group of servers on the Internet. A domain name needs to be registered and a payment is required. It can be used in e-mail addresses or to identify web pages. For example, in the web address http://www.granadalearning.co.uk / the domain name is granadalearning.co.uk.

eg) Ronaldo registered a domain name for his new website.
➡ domain, uniform resource locator (URL)

dotcom
noun

A dotcom is an Internet-based business that aims to make a profit from selling goods or services online.

eg) Amazon is a dotcom that sells books, videos, software and wine.

A B C **D** E F G H I J K L M N O P Q R S T U V W X Y Z

🛈 The name dotcom derives from the way in which the URL is pronounced. So www.amazon.com is pronounced 'amazon dotcom'.
➡ uniform resource locator (URL)

dots per inch [dpi] ✉
noun

Dots per inch (dpi) is the number of spots of ink in each inch of an image.

eg The high dpi meant that the image looked sharp on the page.

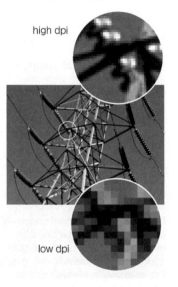

high dpi

low dpi

download 🔍
verb

To download is to copy a file or software to your own computer from another server or source. You can download from a website or a device attached to your computer, such as a digital camera.

eg She downloaded the latest version of the software from the website.

To view the magazine you will need Acrobat reader (click here to download Acrobat) **Get Acrobat Reader**

➡ upload

draft ↩
noun

An early version of a document rather than a final, corrected copy is called a draft.

eg Mr Rogem told the class to write a draft version of their essays before they attempted a final, neat copy.

drag ✉
verb

To drag is to move an object across a computer screen from one place to another by placing the pointer over it, holding down a mouse button and 'dragging' the mouse to a new position. Once in the required position the mouse button can be released and the object 'dropped' into place. This process is usually referred to as 'drag and drop'. Files, images and sections of text can be moved in this way.

eg Ryan decided to drag the picture to a different place in the text.

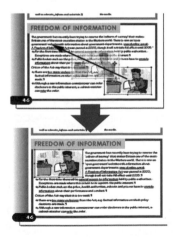

drive ✉
noun

A drive is a device on a computer that can be used to store data. It can be internal or external.

If your computer has a CD-RW drive you can make a copy of data.

➡ **CD-ROM, disk drive, DVD-RW, floppy disk, hard disk drive, storage, zip drive**

driver ✉
noun

A device driver is the software that acts as an interface between your computer and peripheral hardware, such as a printer or disk drive. Drivers are supplied by the manufacturer of the peripheral.

If you don't install the drivers that come with your printer then it won't work when connected to your computer.

➡ **peripheral**

drop-down menu ✉
noun

A drop-down menu offers a range of options and appears when the user clicks on a word in the menu bar. It is, essentially, a menu within a menu. It allows large numbers of options to be presented and prioritised in the minimal amount of space.

He selected the 'Save as Webpage' option from the 'File' drop-down menu.

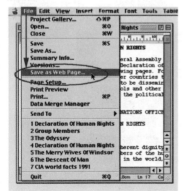

duplicate ✉
noun (verb: to duplicate)

A duplicate of something is a copy of it.

It's a good idea to make a duplicate copy of important files.

DVD
➡ **Digital Video Disk**

DVD-RW ✉
noun/abbreviation

DVD-RW stands for Digital Video Disk Read Write. It is one of the recordable formats for DVDs.

He transferred the video of his sister's wedding to a DVD-RW disk, so that the rest of the family could watch it on their DVD players.

➡ **CD-ROM, Digital Video Disk**

dynamic link ✉
noun

When a smaller program is linked to a larger program we call it a dynamic link. The larger program can call on the smaller program when it needs it to carry out a task. As the smaller program is not needed all of the time, space is saved in the random access memory (RAM) of the computer.

When you are editing a Word document, the printer dynamic link file does not need to be loaded into the computer's random access memory (RAM). But when you decide to print your document then Word causes the printer dynamic link file to be loaded and run. Dynamic link files that support a particular device are known as drivers.

➡ **driver, random access memory (RAM)**

Ee

EAN
➡ **European article number**

earphones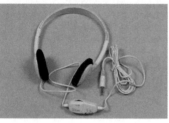
noun (singular: earphone)

Earphones, or headphones, are used to channel sound by placing them into, or over, the ears.

🔵 You won't disturb other passengers on the train if you wear earphones while using your laptop.

e-commerce
noun

When a company sells goods and customers pay for them via a website, this is known as e-commerce.

🔵 The Letts website is an example of e-commerce. You can buy books and CD-ROMs online and pay for them with a credit or debit card.

KS3 Study Guide: Science

SCIENCE

ISBN: 1857589432
List price: £8.99

Add to order

Key Stage 3 is a crucial phase in your education. At there are compulsory National Tests, and important be made about GCSE courses. So this is a vital time

edit ↻
verb

To edit is to correct, improve or make changes to a piece of written work. In word-processing packages the Edit facility on the toolbar can be used to do this.

🔵 Before you put a news item on a website it's a good idea to edit it.
➡ **draft**

effect ✉
noun

An effect is a change made to a picture by using paint or image manipulation software.

🔵 Alice added an art brush effect to the photo of her friend.

A B C D E F G H I J K L M N O P Q R S T U V W X Y Z

26

effective
adjective

An action is effective if it produces the result that was required.

eg Karl produced an effective data handling package. It produced all the lists that the customer wanted and was also very easy to use.

efficient (e-fi-shent)
adjective (noun: efficiency)

If something is efficient then it is effective, and does not require any unnecessary effort.

eg The most efficient way of carrying out the task was to work with two windows open.

electronic funds transfer at point of sale [EFTPOS]
noun

Electronic funds transfer at point of sale, or EFTPOS, is the process which enables a credit card or debit card to be used to pay for goods. A card reader is connected to a telephone line and the amount can be automatically debited.

eg EFTPOS allows people to pay for things without the need to write cheques or carry lots of cash.

e-mail
noun

The word e-mail is an abbreviated version of 'electronic mail'. It is a message composed of text sent electronically between two people.

eg You need an e-mail address to send and receive e-mail.

➡ e-mail address, e-mail attachment, mailbox

e-mail address
noun

An e-mail address is a unique address for an electronic mail box from which e-mails are sent or received.

eg Helen@topediting.co.uk is a typical e-mail address. The first part of the e-mail address refers to the individual or part of the organisation to whom the e-mail is addressed. The second part after the @ symbol is the domain name.

➡ domain name, e-mail, e-mail attachment, Internet service provider (ISP), mailbox

A
B
C
D
E
F
G
H
I
J
K
L
M
N
O
P
Q
R
S
T
U
V
W
X
Y
Z

e-mail attachment ✉
noun

When a file is sent with an e-mail it is known as an e-mail attachment. The file does not open with the e-mail but has to be opened separately. Before you open attachments it is essential to check and see if they contain a virus.

🔵 Mary's sister sent her a picture as an e-mail attachment.

➡ **domain name, e-mail, e-mail address, Internet service provider (ISP), mailbox**

emulator ✉
noun

An emulator is hardware or software that imitates another program or device. It enables you to run software that you would not otherwise be able to run.

🔵 When you run a Windows emulator on your Mac you are able to run all Microsoft software.

enhance 🔄
verb

To enhance is to improve something.

🔵 You can enhance your work by using graphics.

MENU
Thursday 31 October

MAIN MEALS
Spaghetti Bolognese
Pizza
Beefburger
Chilli con carne

VEGETABLES
Baked potato
Mashed potato
Rice
Mixed salad
Peas
Baked beans

DESSERTS
Ice cream
Fresh fruit
Rice pudding

~ MENU ~
Thursday 31 October

~ MAIN MEALS ~
*Spaghetti Bolognese
Pizza
Beefburger
Chilli con carne*

~ VEGETABLES ~
*Baked potato
Mashed potato
Rice
Mixed salad
Peas
Baked beans*

~ DESSERTS ~
*Ice cream
Fresh fruit
Rice pudding*

enquiry 🔍
noun

An enquiry is a question or an investigation.

🔵 She made an enquiry about available hotel accommodation via the website.

enter ✏
verb

To enter is to add or include something.

🔵 The teacher told them to enter the data in the spreadsheet.

European article number [EAN]

noun

A European article number, or EAN, is a type of bar code that includes extra digits for the identification of a country.

eg The EAN is one of many bar code standards used.

➡ bar code, electronic funds transfer at point of sale (EFTPOS)

evaluate
verb

To evaluate is to estimate the worth or value of something.

eg They were asked to evaluate the work they had produced.

evaluation
noun

An evaluation is an assessment of an action. It is often concerned with how effective a solution to a particular problem is.

eg In his evaluation of the software, the customer said that although it did what was needed, it ran rather slowly.

expected outcome
noun

The expected outcome is the result that you would expect to happen at the end.

eg The expected outcome was that they would have greater knowledge of how to manipulate an image.

experiment

verb

To experiment is to try things out.

eg It's a good idea to experiment with different words in a free text search.

export
verb

To export is to save data in a different format, so that it can be used with a different program.

eg He decided to export his address list, so that he could use it with his new mail reader.

➡ import

extrapolate (ex-*tra*-po-layt)
verb

To extrapolate means to use existing knowledge to predict what might or will happen in an unknown situation such as the future.

eg When the Chancellor extrapolated the current figures for public spending into the next three years, he realised that he would have to raise taxes yet again.

A
B
C
D
E
F
G
H
I
J
K
L
M
N
O
P
Q
R
S
T
U
V
W
X
Y
Z

Ff

FAQ
noun/abbreviation

FAQ stands for Frequently Asked Questions. It is a list of the questions and answers that are most commonly asked by people.

eg You will find a FAQ list on websites or on documentation accompanying software.

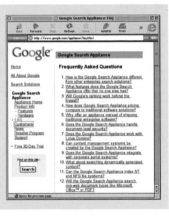

feature (*fee-chur*)
noun

A feature is an element of something which is incorporated into the design.

eg A new feature of the software was that you could store and organise your own photographs.

feedback
noun

When the output from a system is used to influence input, this is called feedback.

eg A computer system opened a window in the greenhouse to lower the temperature. The lowered temperature was detected and this data was sent back to the computer as feedback.

field
noun

A field is an area within a record in a database.

eg A field stores a single item of data about the person or thing that is the subject of the record.

➡ record

file
noun

A file is a store of data on a computer disk or tape. It can be data or a program.

eg Lou worked out his accounts using a spreadsheet and saved the results on disk as a file.

file extension
noun

A file extension is a short name added to the main name of a file to indicate the application that created it. It follows a dot and is usually three or four letters long.

eg The file extension .doc tells you that it is a Word document, while the file extension .xls tells you that it is an Excel document.

samples	
Name ▲	Size
19_2K_CD.MOV	45,888 KB
applicationform.rtf	68 KB
bungle.JPG	378 KB
cat.DXF	3,640 KB
cat.OBJ	1,792 KB
database.doc	318 KB
fore_paws.bgeo	5 KB
ice.TIF	827 KB
JKsoundtrack.wav	39,569 KB

➡ file

file name
noun

A file name is the name you choose to call a file when you save it. Part

A B C D E **F** G H I J K L M N O P Q R S T U V W X Y Z

30

of the file name is the file extension, that comes after the dot. You need to choose file names that indicate the contents, so that you don't have to open the files to see what they contain. 'History homework' is not a good file name if you always do your history homework on the computer. 'History Tudors' might be a better choice.

🔵 The more files he created the more Tom realised it was essential to have a proper system of file names.

➡ **file extension**

file size

noun

File size is measured in bytes. The bigger the number of bytes, the bigger the file, as more data is being stored within it.

🔵 Before sending an attachment it is important to check the file size.

➡ **byte, kilobyte (KB), megabyte (MB)**

find
verb

To find is to look or search for something.

🔵 He used the 'Find' function on his computer to search for the program he needed.

find and replace

noun

Find and replace is a function on word-processing software that enables you to find a word or phrase in the text and replace it with another.

🔵 It was easy to change the name of the character in her story by using find and replace.

fitness for purpose
noun

Something is said to have fitness for purpose if it does the job it is supposed to do.

🔵 They discussed whether the website had fitness for purpose. Did it give people the information they required?

floppy disk

noun

A floppy disk – sometimes called just a floppy – is a removeable storage device that is used for saving data.

🔵 Although they are versatile, you can't store that much data on a floppy disk.

flow chart
noun

A flow chart or flow diagram illustrates the sequence of operations in a procedure.

🔵 A flow diagram is an excellent way of organising your thoughts when planning something.

folder

noun

A folder (also known as a directory) is a container on disk for storing files. It is useful for keeping similar files together.

🔵 When you are setting up a website, it is easiest if you store your images in one folder and your pages in another.

font ✉
noun

A font is a printable or displayable type of text in a particular size.

🥚 Arial is a popular font in e-mails.

font size ✉
noun

Font size is the actual size of the individual characters in text. It is expressed as a number.

🥚 He used a 16 point font size for the heading.

➡ font

Sans serif (e.g. Arial)

ABCDEFGHIJKLMNOPQRSTUVWXYZ
abcdefghijklmnopqrstuvwxyz
1234567890!@£$%^&*()

Serif (e.g. Garamond)

ABCDEFGHIJKLMNOPQRSTUVWXYZ
abcdefghijklmnopqrstuvwxyz
1234567890!@£$%^&*()

Slab serif (e.g. Rockwell)

ABCDEFGHIJKLMNOPQRSTUVWXYZ
abcdefghijklmnopqrstuvwxyz
1234567890!@£$%^&*()

Semi-serif (e.g. Optima)

ABCDEFGHIJKLMNOPQRSTUVWXYZ
abcdefghijklmnopqrstuvwxyz
1234567890!@£$%^&*()

Script (e.g. Nuptial)

ABCDEFGHIJKLMNOPQRSTUVWXYZ
abcdefghijklmnopqrstuvwxyz
1234567890!@£$%^&*()

Dingbats (e.g. Zapf Dingbats)

Fancy (e.g. Wonton)

ABCDEFGHIJKLMNOPQRSTUVWXYZ
abcdefghijklmnopqrstuvwxyz
1234567890!@£$%^&*()

Roman	Italic
AaBbCc	*AaBbCc*
Bold	**Bold italic**
AaBbCc	***AaBbCc***

Font sizes

Aa 10pt Aa 12pt Aa 18pt Aa 24pt Aa 36pt

footer
noun

A footer is text or an image displayed at the foot or bottom of every page of a document.

🔵 If you wish to add a footer to a document then click on the 'View' option on the toolbar.

➡ **header**

footnote
noun

A note at the bottom of a page, commenting in more detail on a point in the text is a footnote.

🔵 A footnote can be used to clarify the meaning of a word used in the body text.

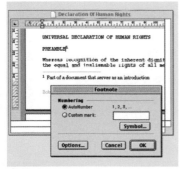

➡ **footer**

forecast
verb

To forecast is to predict what will happen.

🔵 When designing the sequence of instructions the pupils had to forecast how the robot would respond.

format
noun

The format is the way in which the data is set out in a file. Different kinds of formats include bitmap, numeric data and text.

🔵 He changed the file to rich text format.
➡ **bitmap**

formatting
noun (verb: to format)

Formatting is the process of changing the appearance of a document. This may be done by changing the font, margins, borders, shading or background.

🔵 Arthur used formatting to change the plain text into a poster.
➡ **document formatting**

formula
noun (plural: formulae)

A formula is an equation used to find quantities when given certain values. A formula can be used in a spreadsheet.

🔵 The formula for adding the 3 values in the spreadsheet was =A4+A5+A6.

forum
noun

An online discussion group where individuals post messages is known as a forum.

🔵 He used the forum as a way of asking for information.

A
B
C
D
E

F

G
H
I
J
K
L
M
N
O
P
Q
R
S
T
U
V
W
X
Y
Z

frequency (*free-cwen-see*)
noun

The number of times that something happens is called the frequency.

eg The frequency of people using the Internet is greater in the evenings.

frequency diagram
noun

A frequency diagram is an illustration of the frequency of a given event.

eg The frequency diagram showed when usage of the website was the heaviest.

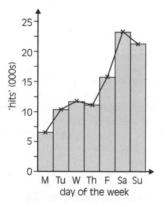

functional (*funk-shun-al*)
adjective

If something is functional it is efficiently serving its purpose.

eg They tested to see if the search engine was functional.

gateway
noun

A gateway is a computer linking two different networks.

eg A computer at your Internet service provider acts as a gateway.

➡ network

gigabyte
noun

A gigabyte is a unit of computer storage. It is 1024 MB (megabytes). This is the same as 1 073 741 824 bytes. This is more than a billion bytes.

eg The latest PC in our range has 256 megabytes of RAM and a 200 gigabyte hard drive.

External Drives

Model	Size	Order No
HiDrive40	40GB	HD40X
CoppIT-H2	120GB	HD120X
Gass/R25	250GB	HD250X

Internal Drives

Model	Size	Order No.
HiDriveA2	40GB	HD40IN
HiDriveA92	120GB	HD120IN
HiDriveB2	250GB	HD250IN

➡ bit, byte, megabyte (MB)

goal seek
noun

Goal seek is a function in spreadsheet software. You can specify the final answer you want and the program works backwards to find the input values that produce the answer you have specified.

eg If you want to save a particular sum of money then you can use goal seek to work out how much you need to invest each month.

graph (*graaf*)
noun

A graph is a way of illustrating a relationship between variables.

eg A graph was drawn to show how much they had raised each month for charity.

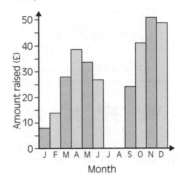

Month

graphics (*gra-fics*)
noun

Graphics are pictures on a computer display.

eg In the past, some computers were not able to display graphics.

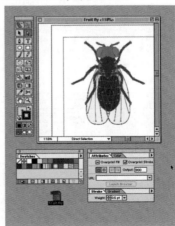

35

A
B
C
D
E
F
G
H
I
J
K
L
M
N
O
P
Q
R
S
T
U
V
W
X
Y
Z

graphics interchange format [GIF]
noun

A Graphics Interchange Format (GIF) file is a compressed graphics file used for images on the Internet.

eg GIF files are used by web designers for animated images.

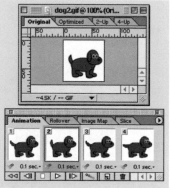

➡ **World Wide Web**

gridlines
noun (singular: grid line)

Gridlines are a feature of any kind of table. They are used to present data to users in an organised way on the screen.

eg You can hide the gridlines of a table in a word-processing package.

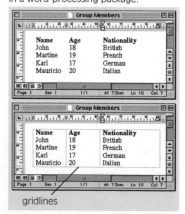

gridlines

grouped data
noun

Most sets of data contain a range of values. To make the information easier to analyse, it can be organised into a number of smaller ranges, or intervals. Data organised into smaller intervals in this way is called grouped data.

eg The grouped data had intervals of 5 cm.

Hh

hacking
noun (verb: to hack)

Hacking is now used by the media to describe any illegal or unauthorised access to a computer system. However, it can be used to describe a quick way of dealing with a problem with a program.

eg The company spent a considerable amount of money to protect itself against hacking.

➡ **computer crime, virus**

hard disk drive
noun

The hard disk drive is the magnetic storage device for a computer. Its capacity is measured in gigabytes. It reads and writes data.

eg The hard disk drive can be found inside your computer but you can also buy an external hard drive.

hardware
noun

Hardware is the name for all physical aspects of computing such as screens, power units, cables, mouse and printers. It is different from software which is the name for programs you run on your computer.

eg He extended the hardware of his computer by buying a scanner and a printer.

header
noun

A header is text or an image displayed at the head or top of every page of a document.

eg If you wish to add a header to a document then click on the 'View' option on the toolbar.

➡ **footer**

heading
noun

The heading is the title of the whole or a section of a document.

eg You can put your heading in bold and underline it to make it stand out.

hierarchical (*hire-ar-ki-kal*)
adjective

Something is hierarchical if it is arranged in a graded order. A hierarchical system is a way of organising files so that you can easily find them later. For example, the files can be organised by topic or the type of format.

eg A tree structure is the most common hierarchical system.

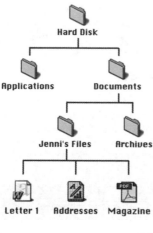

Hard Disk

Applications   Documents

Jenni's Files   Archives

Letter 1   Addresses   Magazine

hits
noun (singular: hit)

Hits are the number of visits to a website.

eg More hits to your website means that more people have looked at it.

home page
noun

The home page is the main page of a website that usually lists the contents. It is also the name given to an individual's personal website.

eg Andy added the new photo to her home page.

hot spot
noun

A hot spot is any part of a screen display that is activated in response to mouse clicks.

eg He clicked on the hot spot and made the image move.

hyperlink
noun

A hyperlink is text or an image in a web page with particular formatting. When you click on a hyperlink you are taken to a different part of that web page or to another web page.

eg With a hyperlink you can direct the user of a web page to the next important piece of information.

- The latest information for Higher Education reviews of universities in the UK.
- The most respected careers guides in the titles from Trotman Publishing to choose f bookshop.
- UCAS form advice and information to mak right first time.
- The CV builder - find all the information yo CV that stands out from the rest.
- Advice for job interviews - hints and tips th the ideal interviewee!

➔ **hypertext**

hypertext

noun

Sometimes, the text you see on a computer screen contains words that are highlighted. When you click on a highlighted word, you are taken to another place in the document or possibly a website. This kind of text is called hypertext.

🔵 The help pages for the wordprocessor were written in hypertext, so when Julie clicked on a word, an explanation of the word was displayed.

hypertext mark-up language [HTML]
noun

Hypertext mark-up language (HTML) is the code in which websites are written. Your browser will read the code and turn it into the text you see on screen.

🔵 When you are looking at a web page you can easily see the HTML it is based on. Just click 'View' on the menu and then 'Source'.

➡ **web browser**

hypothesis
noun

A hypothesis is an assumption that you try out or test, to see whether it is true or false.

🔵 He tested out the hypothesis that the virus had been spread by e-mail.

A
B
C
D
E
F
G
H
I
J
K
L
M
N
O
P
Q
R
S
T
U
V
W
X
Y
Z

Ii

identify
verb

To identify is to find something or to describe what something is.

eg We need to identify the users of the website before we start to design it.

if...then
noun

If...then is the name of a command sequence. If...then checks something (usually a value) and then tells the program how to proceed.

eg If the man is green then cross the road. If x = 10 then end the program.

illustration (i-lus-tray-shun)
noun

A way of explaining something either by using pictures or examples is an illustration.

eg By way of illustration he added a picture of the house to the description of it.

image (i-midge)
noun

An image is a picture or representation of something.

eg He downloaded the image from his digital camera to his computer.

import
verb

To import is to bring data into one program when it was originally created in another.

eg It is possible to import data into a spreadsheet from the Internet.
➡ export

improve
verb

To improve is to make something better than it was before.

eg He wanted to improve his skills in website design.

index
noun

An index is an alphabetical list of contents found at the end of a book. It is also used to refer to any alphabetical list of contents, such as that found in the 'Help' section on software.

eg He searched in the index for the information he required.

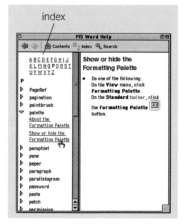

index

information (in-for-may-shun)
noun

Information is a set of facts or data, which has been interpreted so that it has meaning for humans.

eg The data processed by the computer was a set of numbers: 120303. When this data was printed out in the report, it was displayed as 12th March 2003, which was the information that Jo wanted.
➡ data

information source
noun

An information source is the place where you find something out.

eg The teacher told them they were to use more than one information source when writing their essay.

input
1 noun

The data that is given to a computer to process is called the input. Input devices are used to convert the input into the electrical signals that the computer can use.

eg The greenhouse control system used the temperature as the input.

2 verb

To input is to feed data into a computer for processing. When you type on a keyboard you are inputting data.

eg The data was first collected on the application forms and then input into the database.

➡ output

input device
noun

An input device is a piece of hardware used to enter data or commands into a computer program.

eg The keyboard, mouse and joystick are all examples of input devices.

➡ input, output

intended audience
noun

The people who it is expected will read a document, use a website or listen to a presentation are the intended audience.

eg The intended audience for the medical website was doctors rather than the general public.

international services digital network [ISDN]
noun

International services digital network, or ISDN, is a high-speed way of transmitting digital data through either a copper telephone wire or optic fibre cable.

eg If you have ISDN installed in your home then you won't need a modem.

➡ broadband

Internet
noun

The Internet is a world-wide network of connected computers. It has been able to grow because all the computers communicate in the same way. It includes millions of web pages, known as the World Wide Web. It also allows people to send e-mails and transfer data across the world.

eg Joe found out the price of an airline ticket by searching websites on the Internet.

The Internet was originally created by the US military, and was then used by universities before being opened up to the public. Very few people were able to spot the potential of the Internet when it first came out. Bill Gates, of Microsoft, said in 1993, 'The Internet? We are not interested in it.'

➡ World Wide Web

Internet service provider [ISP]
noun

An Internet service provider (ISP) is a company that provides access to the Internet, e-mail and web hosting services for the

A B C D E F G H I J K L M N O P Q R S T U V W X Y Z

public. They usually make a charge for this service.

🔧 There are many different services offered by ISPs and it is wise to check exactly what you will be getting for your money. The two main services offered by ISPs are unlimited access through a dial up connection or a broadband connection. The dial up connection is cheaper but it does tie up your telephone line. The broadband connection is more expensive, but it has the advantages of being quicker and always available.

eg Before you sign up with an ISP it is a good idea to read a review of their service on the Internet.

➡ e-mail, Internet

interpolate
verb

To interpolate is to predict other results within given values.

eg The student's shoe sizes were plotted against heights in a scatter graph and a line of best fit was drawn. This enabled Gillian to interpolate the shoe sizes for other students of different heights.

interrogate
verb

To interrogate a database is to explore its contents.

eg Romola decided to interrogate the database to find out how many items were in each group.

intranet
noun

An intranet is a network of computers, similar to the Internet, but it is only accessible to a single organisation or group of people.

eg Each subject had a shared area on the school intranet.

➡ Internet

ISDN
➡ international services digital network

italic
noun

Italic is a sloping style of text used for special emphasis in documents. The option to make text italic appears on the tool bar of word-processing software.

eg Kim used italic text for all the important words in her essay.

🔧 Italic text was invented in Italy. It can be used to make words *stand out,* either for emphasis or because they are from a foreign language. Sometimes you will see italic text used for quotations or used instead of brackets.

Jj

Java ✉
noun

Java is a programming language especially written for use in designing web pages. Small Java applications are called Java applets.

eg Java applets in web pages allow users to interact with the page. You can see Java applets loading at the bottom of your browser.

➡ **hypertext mark-up language (HTML)**

JPEG ✉
noun/abbreviation

JPEG stands for Joint Photographic Experts Group. It is a compressed graphic file format for displaying photographs on the Internet. The filename extension is .JPG.

eg Caleph saved the image as a medium quality JPEG file.

➡ **Graphics Interchange Format (GIF)**

judge 🔗
verb

To judge is to assess the qualities of something.

eg It was time to judge the most successful website in the class.

key word
noun

A key word is an important word in a web page that describes its content. The key word makes searching for the document much easier. Key words are meta-tags written into the HTML of a web page.

eg The key words for the census website were, 'census' and 'online'.

➡ content, hypertext mark-up language (HTML), meta-tags, search engine

keyboard
noun

A keyboard is an input device, linked to your computer and made up of individual keys, that can be used to input data and commands.

eg If you use your keyboard incorrectly then you could get repetitive strain injury.

🗈 The main keyboard in the English speaking world is the Qwerty keyboard. It is called this after the first 6 letters on the left-hand side of the keyboard. It was developed by Christoper Scholes in 1873 for the manual typewriter. Originally the keys were arranged alphabetically, but this led to the keys jamming as people typed too quickly. So Scholes solved the problem by placing certain keys far apart on the keyboard.

➡ input device

kilobyte [KB]
noun

A kilobyte is a unit of computer storage and is approximately a thousand bytes or 1024 bytes to be precise.

eg He looked at the attachment and noted that it was 334 kilobytes in size.

➡ byte, gigabyte, megabyte

label
noun

A label is a word or small amount of text added to a diagram to give extra information. The label text is usually linked to the appropriate part of the diagram by a line.

eg If you add a label to a diagram it will make things clearer for the reader.

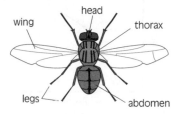

wing   head   thorax
legs   abdomen

landscape
adjective

Landscape is one of the options you can use when you print a document or image. When you choose landscape the page is printed horizontally. In software you can find this option by going to 'File' then 'Page Setup'.

eg If you are printing an image that is wider rather than it is tall, you will probably want your image printed in landscape mode.

➡ portrait

laptop
noun

A laptop is a portable computer consisting of screen, keyboard and a CD-ROM drive. It can be run using batteries as well as mains electricity.

eg A laptop is more convenient than a desktop computer as you can use it almost anywhere.

50 years ago it was difficult for people to imagine that a powerful computer with a range of applications could be a portable device that people could carry around with them. Computers were heavy, difficult to move and took up a whole room. As the magazine *Popular Mechanics* said in 1949, 'In the future, computers may weigh no more that 1.5 tonnes.'

➡ **desktop computer**

layered objects
noun

When pictures and items of text are placed one on top of another on a page, they are called layered objects.

eg The layered objects on the advertisement were: a picture of the phone, the price and the company logo.

PRICES FROM
£19.99

mobes2go

layering

noun

In graphics, layering is the process of placing several objects on to a background, over or under each other. An image created in a graphics application is made up of different layers. If you imagine an image of a sunset, the orange background may be one layer, next the drifting clouds and then the sun. When they are seen together to create a picture of a sunset we say the objects have been layered.

🅴🅶 Layering is an important skill to develop when using graphic applications. Images produced by digital means are easier to adapt and manipulate using layers because the artist/designer is able to work on separate layers, such as the background, without disturbing other elements. When you are satisfied with the picture, the layers may be combined and saved as an image.

layout

noun

Layout is the way in which different individual items are arranged, and how they work together on a page.

🅴🅶 An understanding of basic page layout is essential for building effective web pages.

➡ page view

length delimited file
noun

When the records in a file have a predetermined size, which does not vary, it is said to be a length delimited file. If 20 bytes are reserved for someone's surname and you enter 'Smith', only 5 bytes will be used, the other 15 are wasted.

🅴🅶 Amy set up the data table so that each record was 100 bytes in size. It was a length delimited file so she knew that 10 records would always take up 1000 bytes on the disk.

line of best fit

noun

The line of best fit is drawn approximately in the middle of the points of a scatter diagram. It enables you to estimate values not given in the original information.

🅴🅶 The students' shoe sizes were plotted against heights in a scatter graph and a line of best fit was drawn.

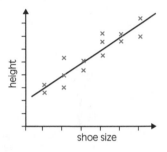

➡ scatter graph

link

noun

A link is a connection. The word 'link' is often used as a shortened version of 'hyperlink', to give the name of a connection you can follow to another page or website.

🅴🅶 He followed the link to the World War I history site.

➡ hyperlink

live data
noun

Live data is up-to-date data that is immediately available.

🅴🅶 The students accessed the website for live data on volcano activity.

load
verb

To load is to transfer data or a program to the computer's main memory. You will often see the message 'loading' at the bottom of your browser while you wait for a website to download.

eg You need to learn how to load software to get the most out of your computer.

local area network [LAN]
noun

A local area network is a system for connecting computers together so they can share software, files and documents. The local area network covers a single building or others close to it.

eg Most schools have a local area network (LAN).

➡ wide area network (WAN)

locate
verb

To locate is to find.

eg The class were told to locate the browser on their desktop.

location
noun

The location is a place where you find something.

eg He tried to find the location of the file on his computer.

➡ locate

Logo
noun

Logo is a programming language devised for school children to teach thinking and programming skills.

eg Logo uses a turtle to move around the screen.

➡ control

logo
noun

A logo is a small symbol or design used to represent a company.

eg Some logos are widely recognised around the world. This is the Letts logo.

log off
verb

To log off is to finish using a computer system, usually by clicking on 'Shutdown'. You may also be asked to log off or log out from a website when you have finished using it.

eg The class were told to log off as it was the end of the lesson.

➡ log on

log on
verb

To log on is to gain access to a computer system, usually by entering your name and password. You may also be asked to log in to a website by giving a user name and password.

eg At the start of the lesson the teacher told the class to log on.

➡ log off

lower case
adjective

The lower case letters are the small letters of the alphabet, rather than the capital or uppercase letters.

eg The company used lower case letters on its corporate logo.

➡ upper case

mailbox
noun

A mailbox can be found within mail manager software such as Outlook Express. You can save e-mails from different people in separate mailboxes and give each box a name which enables you to find them easily and quickly.

eg Rupert had a mailbox for his friends' e-mails and a mailbox for his family e-mails.

➡ mail manager

mail manager
noun

A mail manager or mail reader is the type of software used for sending and receiving e-mails.

eg Outlook Express and Entourage are examples of mail managers.

➡ e-mail, mailbox

mail merge
noun

Mail merge enables the same letter to be individually addressed to different people by linking it to a database of names and addresses. Most word processing packages have a mail merge facility.

eg The secretary of the swimming club used mail merge to send out a letter to each of the members.

manipulate
verb

To manipulate is to change how something looks.

eg They were taught how to manipulate images in Photoshop.

mean
noun

The mean, or arithmetic mean, is an average value found by dividing the sum of a set of quantities by the number of quantities.

eg The mean is one kind of average.

➡ median, mode

median (*mee-dee-an*)
noun

The median is the middle item in an ascending sequence of items.

eg The class were told to find the median in the list of numbers.

➡ mean, mode

megabyte [MB]
noun

A megabyte is approximately a million bytes and precisely 1,048,576 bytes. You can also think of it as 1024 kilobytes.

eg He knew that the attachment was large as it was one megabyte in size.

➡ byte, kilobyte

menu
noun

When a computer user is offered a series of options while using software these options are known as a menu. The menu is usually found on the menu bar at the top of the screen or window. Using a mouse, the user can move a highlighted bar and then make a choice from the menu.

eg Lucy selected the 'Undo Typing' option from the 'Edit' menu on Word.

🎌 Software that follows the guidelines for Microsoft's Windows usually starts from the left with the menu options 'File', 'Edit', 'View'.

This makes it easier for users when they come to use different types of software.

metadata

noun

Metadata is data about data, such as who produced it and when it was written, rather than the actual data itself. Metadata is used in XML so that searching for specific content on the Internet is easier.

eg The web page contained the following metadata: 'author', 'date of publication' and 'title'.

ℹ Metadata is the modern term for the kind of information that museums and libraries have traditionally entered into their catalogues about their resources. The word metadata is mainly used to refer to descriptive information about resources on the Internet. Individual pieces of metadata are called meta-tags, or just tags.

➡ meta-tags, XML

meta-tags

noun (singular: meta-tag)

Meta-tags are key words in HTML describing the important contents of a web page. They are placed near the beginning of the HTML version of the page and are found by search engines looking for any of the content described. Meta-tags are sometimes just called tags.

eg Well-written meta-tags can help make pages rank higher in search results.

```
<html>               meta-tag
   <meta name="keywords"
content="John Smith homepage
football Manchester United">

   <body>
      <table border="0"
cellpadding="4" cellspacing="0"
```

➡ hypertext mark-up language (HTML), key word, tags

microphone

noun

A microphone is a device used for recording sound.

eg Attaching a microphone to your computer allows you to add sound to your presentations.

misrepresentation

noun

A misrepresentation is an untrue or misleading version of something.

eg You need to check that a web page does not give a misrepresentation of the facts.

misuse

verb

To misuse something is to use it for the wrong purpose.

eg If you misuse a chat room then you are likely to get banned from it.

mode

noun

The mode is the average value that is most frequent.

eg 6 is the mode of the following values; 5, 3, 6, 9, 6, 8, 1, 6.

➡ mean, median

model

noun

A model is a representation of a real object or event. It is usually a set of mathematical rules and relationships and can be programmed on a computer. A model can be used to construct a simulation of a real event.

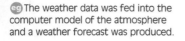

eg The weather data was fed into the computer model of the atmosphere and a weather forecast was produced.

moderate ✉
verb

To moderate something is to keep it within the rules or boundaries.

eg The forum was moderated and abusive postings were removed.
➡ netiquette

monitor
1 verb

To monitor is to watch over the progress of something.

eg You need to monitor your action plan to ensure that you are keeping to schedule.

2 noun

A monitor is another name for a visual display unit such as a computer screen.

mouse ✉
noun

A mouse is an input device, controlled by movements of the hand. A pointer on the screen moves in response to the hand's movements. When you click on the mouse it selects the object you are pointing to on the screen.

eg Jay used a double-click on the mouse to select the text he wanted to highlight.

The plural of mouse is mice. Douglas Englebart is usually regarded as the inventor of the mouse in the 1960s. However, the first commercial version did not come out until 1982.
➡ input device

moving image ✉
noun

A moving image, such as a video or film, is one that gives the appearance of action. In fact, all moving images are made up of many static pictures, played back in a rapid sequence.

eg Jamie wanted a moving image for her presentation, but had to use a photo instead.

MP3 ✉
noun/abbreviation

MP3 is the file extension for audio layer 3 of MPEG. It is a format for compressing sound files. This means that the files are smaller and easier to transfer.

eg He bought himself a personal stereo that could play MP3 files he had found on the band's website.

At one time it was possible for individuals to offer their MP3 music files over the Internet through

companies such as Napster. However in 2001, breach of copyright suits from the music companies prevented this. It is still possible to obtain copyright-free MP3 files over the Internet – just visit the official website of a band.
➡ copyright

multimedia authoring
noun ✉

Multimedia authoring is the process of using software to create a presentation that involves sound, moving and still images, and text.

eg Macromedia Director is a popular multimedia authoring tool.
➡ multimedia presentation

multimedia presentation
noun ✉

A multimedia presentation uses software to create a presentation that involves sound, moving and still images.

eg A multimedia presentation can be used on a website.
➡ multimedia authoring

Nn

navigate
verb

To navigate is to find your way around.

In ICT we talk about websites being easy to navigate.

netiquette (ne-ti-ket)
noun

Netiquette refers to the informal set of rules which you have to keep to when using the Internet. It applies particularly to using newsgroups, chat rooms and forums.

Not making abusive postings to forums is an example of netiquette.

This word derives from the combination of network (as in Internet), and the French word 'etiquette'. There have always been conventions and rules about how people speak and write to each other. When the Internet became more popular people soon realised they needed a set of rules for communicating in this new medium. This led to the growth of netiquette.

➡ newsgroup

network
noun

A network is a group of computers connected together so that they can share the same data, software and peripherals.

Networks can rely on cables or wireless.

➡ local area network, wide area network

newbie (new-bee)
noun

A newbie is the name for a new user of a newsgroup, forum or bulletin board.

Archie introduced himself as a newbie when he made his first posting to the forum.

The term newbie originally had negative connotations as in 'I wish that newbie would read the netiquette before posting to this newsgroup.' However, a new user of a forum or newsgroup will often introduce themselves as a newbie; this is probably done to forestall any criticism if they unintentionally infringe the netiquette of the group.

➡ newsgroup, netiquette, post

newsgroup
noun

A newsgroup is a discussion forum based around a particular interest or topic. You have to register and subscribe to it.

Outlook Express or another mail manager will give you a list of newsgroups you can subscribe to.

NOT

noun

NOT is a Boolean connector and is one of the options on an advanced search engine. It allows you to leave out certain words on the search. This means that the search is more likely to find the pages you require. On the search engine Google, the 'NOT' option is called 'without the words'.

🔵 If you're looking for sites on 'Birmingham history' in the UK, you can exclude the sites on Birmingham Alabama in the USA, by entering 'Alabama' in the 'NOT' option.

➡ **AND, Boolean, OR, search engine**

numeric
adjective

Something is said to be numeric if it only contains numbers and decimal points.

🔵 You can enter numeric data into a spreadsheet.

A
B
C
D
E
F
G
H
I
J
K
L
M
N
O
P
Q
R
S
T
U
V
W
X
Y
Z

Oo

object

noun

An object is a component part of computer software. All modern software is built from objects. Big objects are often built from smaller objects. A spreadsheet is an object. It is made from smaller objects such as worksheets, buttons, cells and menus.

eg Sinitta placed two objects onto her web form: a text box where people could type their opinions and a button to click in order to send the comments to her e-mail address.

onscreen viewing

noun

Onscreen viewing is the process of reading information from the monitor in front of you.

eg He opened the file containing the image for on-screen viewing.

operating system

noun

The operating system is the main piece of software in your computer that allows you to run all of your other software. The operating system is loaded automatically, or booted, when you switch on your computer. When you buy a computer the operating system is usually already installed for you.

eg Windows 98, Windows 2000, MAC OS X and Linux are all examples of operating systems.

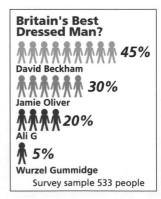

➡ hardware, software

operator

noun

In Maths an operator is a character that stands for an operation. For example + represents addition. In computing a Boolean operator, normally called a Boolean connector, is a way of searching for information more effectively on the Internet.

eg He used the Boolean operator 'OR' to widen to his search to 'Elvis' OR 'Presley'.
➡ AND, Boolean connector, OR, NOT

opinion

noun

An opinion is a view.

eg He was asked for his opinion on the teams most likely to be relegated from the Premiership.

opinion poll

noun

An opinion poll is a survey of people's points of view on different matters. It is carried out by asking questions.

eg The results of the opinion poll showed that David Beckham was judged to be the best dressed man in Britain.

Britain's Best Dressed Man?

👤👤👤👤👤👤👤👤👤 **45%**
David Beckham

👤👤👤👤👤👤 **30%**
Jamie Oliver

👤👤👤👤 20%
Ali G

👤 5%
Wurzel Gummidge

Survey sample 533 people

optical character recognition [OCR]
noun

Optical Character Recognition is the ability of a computer to recognise handwritten or printed text.

eg The post that is delivered to your door has been sorted by Optical Character Recognition machines.

OR
noun

OR is one of the Boolean connectors and is a way of widening your search for web pages using the advanced search option. It allows you to find sites which include at least one of the terms you specify.

eg If you type 'chocolate OR chips' in the search engine then it will find pages with either of the words.

➡ **AND, Boolean connector, NOT**

organise
verb

To organise something is to put it into order.

eg You must set up a system on your computer to organise the files you create or you will have difficulty finding them again.

origin (o-ri-jin)
noun

The origin is where something comes from.

eg The origin of the present day Internet was the US military in the 1960s.
➡ **originator**

originator (o-ri-ji-**nay**-tor)
noun

The originator is the person who comes up with the first, the original, idea.

eg With his invention of calculating machines in the 1820s, Charles Babbage can be said to be the originator of the modern computer.
➡ **origin**

outline view
noun

The outline view is one of the different views you can have of a document that you are writing on a word-processing package. The outline view shows only the basic structure of the document – headers, footers, graphics – and page boundaries do not appear. You use outline view when you want to work on the structure of your document, for example, moving headings and text around.

eg To see the outline view of a document you need to click on 'View' in the menu bar and select 'Outline View'.

➡ **page view**

output
noun

When a computer has finished processing the data that has been input, it gives the results back as output. Output may be sent to the user or to an automatic device.

eg The output from the database was a printed list of all the class members.

output device
noun

An output device is an item of hardware that is used to give the results of computer processing to the user.

eg A printer is the output device that produces hard copy on paper.

A B C D E F G H I J K L M N O P Q R S T U V W X Y Z

Pp

page impression
noun

A page impression is the number of times that a page of a website is requested by users. It is a measurement of the usage of a website, usually for commercial purposes.

eg The website had over a thousand page impressions a day in a three-week period.

page view
noun

The page view is one of the views you have of a document when using word-processing software. It is sometimes called page layout view. You use page view to see how text and graphics will appear on the final printed page. It is also useful for working with margins and for drawing.

eg To see the page view of a document you need to click on 'View' in the menu bar and select 'Page View'.

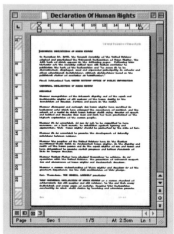

paint and draw software
noun

Paint and draw software is a type of program that allows you to create images. It has features associated with painting such as brushes, filters and colour effects. The drawing features enable you to create and manipulate lines.

eg ClarisWorks incorporates both paint and draw software.

password
noun

A password is a word or phrase that allows you to use a network or a particular website. It is often used in addition to a user name. The use of passwords ensures that data in a website can be kept secure from unauthorised users.

eg The password for the website was 'hotlip'.

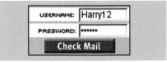

paste
verb

To paste means to stick down. In computing, to paste is to insert text or images into a document after they have been copied or cut from elsewhere. The entire process is usually referred to as cut and paste or copy and paste. The instruction 'Paste' can be found under the 'Edit' menu in software and also on the tool bar as a symbol.

eg You can copy and paste between different programs. The text or image is kept on the clipboard on your computer.

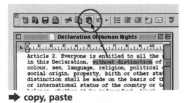

→ copy, paste

patch (*pach*)
noun ✉

A patch is a quick repair program for a piece of software where the programming is faulty and needs to be rectified. Software developers release a patch when a bug has been identified in software.

eg It is a good idea to check the website for any software you own, to see if a patch has been released to deal with a bug.

→ bug

pattern
noun

A pattern is a model or something that you copy.

eg They were given a pattern for the instructions which they had to copy.

peripheral (*pe-ri-fer-al*)
noun

A peripheral is a device that is not a part of the main computer i.e. the memory or microprocessor. Printers and CD-ROM drives are examples of peripherals.

eg If you connect a peripheral to your computer, you will usually have to install software with drivers in order for it to work.

? The word peripheral is used as an adjective to describe something incidental or not that important. The word was adopted by computing as an adjective to describe devices such as printers or scanners that were not the main part of the computer – these are called peripheral devices. However, the word is now used by itself as a noun, in both the plural and singular form, as in 'Have you got many peripherals connected to your computer?'

permissions (*per-mi-shuns*)
noun (singular: permission) ✉

Permissions are different levels of access given to a computer's user, usually on a network. The network administrator can stipulate that certain files are read only for certain users while others have read and write permission.

eg The files in the shared area of the network had read only permissions for pupils and read and write permissions for staff.

personal computer [PC]
noun

A personal computer is a computer designed for one person to use. It usually consists of a monitor, processor unit, keyboard, mouse and often a printer. It can be linked to other computers in a network.

eg Her mother bought her a PC so that she could complete her homework more effectively.

? In July 2002 a report estimated that since the mid-1970s approximately one billion PCs have been sold throughout the world. 75% of these machines have gone into the workplace, while the other 25% have been for use in the

A B C D E F G H I J K L M N O **P** Q R S T U V W X Y Z

home. Of these approximately 81.5% have been desktops. Few people foresaw this phenomenal growth in PC ownership. In 1943 Thomas Watson, chairman of IBM, said 'I think there is a world market for maybe five computers'.

personal digital assistant [PDA]
noun

A Personal Digital Assistant (PDA) is a hand-held computer, usually containing an address book, diary, spreadsheet, word-processing software and sometimes an e-mail facility. Data can be recorded on the move and then synchronised with another computer such as a desktop.

eg Hand-held and palmtop are other names for a PDA.

personal information
noun

Personal information is information about an individual that can be used to identify them. It usually includes a name, possibly an address and other details unique to that person.

eg When ordering goods over the Internet you have to supply personal information, so you must check that the website is secure.
➡ **Data Protection Act**

physical data
noun

Physical data concerns the physical environment such as temperature, pressure or light.

eg The inputs to my system are in the form of physical data: the temperature and light level in the greenhouse.
➡ **data**

photograph (fo-to-graf)
noun

A photograph is a picture made by using a camera.

eg He scanned in the photograph so that he could edit it on his computer.
➡ **scanner**

picture
noun

A picture is a drawing, painting or photograph.

eg You can insert a picture in your document to illustrate what you are trying to say.

pie chart
noun

A pie chart is a circular graph for representing statistical data.

eg The data in the spreadsheet on favourite colours was turned into a pie chart.

Favourite colours

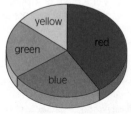

pixel
noun

A pixel is one of the dots on a computer screen that makes up a picture.

eg The physical size of a pixel depends on how you've set your display screen.

pixellated
adjective

Pixellated is a word used to describe an image made up of pixels, each of which is a single point.

🔵 How a pixellated image appears on a display screen depends on its resolution, which is the number of pixels it displays. Some display 300,000 pixels, some 480,000 pixels, while a true colour system displays more than 16 million different colours.

➡ **pixel**

plan 🔗
noun

A plan is a method of achieving something that you set out in advance.

🔵 It takes time, but it is always worth making a plan before you start your work.

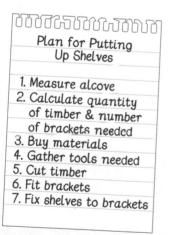

Plan for Putting Up Shelves

1. Measure alcove
2. Calculate quantity of timber & number of brackets needed
3. Buy materials
4. Gather tools needed
5. Cut timber
6. Fit brackets
7. Fix shelves to brackets

➡ **planning frame**

planning frame 🔗
noun

A planning frame for a given task is a grid providing space for notes on a number of topics. You can use a planning frame to organise your thoughts, and then use it as a guide when producing the final piece of work.

🔵 The teacher gave the class a planning frame for their essay on home computing.

plausible (*plaw-si-bul*) 🔗
adjective

If something is plausible then it is achievable or believable.

🔵 With the teacher's help they decided that setting up their own website was a plausible idea.

plug-in
noun

A plug-in is a small program that adds extra capability to an existing program. Plug-ins are usually free and can be downloaded from a website.

🔵 When visiting a website he was directed to another site where he could download a plug-in which he would need. The image below is a screenshot of VersionTracker.com showing Macromedia Flash Player downloads.

points
noun (singular: point)

Points are opinions or facts expressed by people.

🔵 They were given a list of points to include in their essays.

A
B
C
D
E
F
G
H
I
J
K
L
M
N
O
P
Q
R
S
T
U
V
W
X
Y
Z

point of sale [POS]
noun

Point of sale is the place where you buy things, such as a shop or website. A point of sale terminal is a combined cash register and network computer, which logs transactions and can be linked to a database of stock.

➡ **electronic funds transfer at point of sale (EFTPOS)**

pop-up
noun

A pop-up is a small window that appears in your browser when visiting a website, usually containing an advertisement.

🔵 On some browsers there is a suppress pop-up facility.

➡ **pop-up menu**

pop-up menu
noun

A pop-up menu appears on your display screen at the point where your mouse is positioned. It is usually activated by a right-side mouse click.

🔵 Right-click on the mouse to see a pop-up menu.

ISBN: 184085605X
List price: £3.50

Internet Explorer Help...
Open Image in New Window
Download Image to Disk
Copy Image
Reload Image

Letts Success ... ision students remember key information more easily and suc

➡ **pop-up**

port
noun

A port is a connector on the outside of your computer to which you can attach peripheral devices such as a keyboard, mouse, or digital camera.

🔵 You may have a range of ports on your computer such as a parallel, firewire or USB.

portrait
adjective

Portrait is one of the options when you print a document or image. When you choose portrait the page is printed vertically. In software you can find this option by going to 'File' then 'Page Setup'.

🔵 If you have an image that is taller rather than wide, and you want your image to be printed vertically choose 'Portrait'. Portrait is usually the default setting of your printer options.

Table of Results

➡ **landscape**

post
1 noun

A post is a message placed on a newsgroup, forum or online bulletin board.

🔵 Bill's post to the forum concerned a problem he had found while using the software.

2 verb

To post is to place a message on a newsgroup, forum or online bulletin board.

eg Sally decided to post in reply to the message from Bill.

i The word 'post' originally referred to letters delivered to your door by a postman. The word was adopted by the online community to refer to electronic messages. This is an example of how developing technology takes suitable existing words and uses them for a different purpose in a slightly different way.

➡ **forum, newsgroup**

predict
verb

To predict is to judge what will happen on the basis of some evidence.

eg The group had to predict how the robot would move in response to their instructions.

➡ **prediction**

prediction (*pre-dik-shun*)
noun

A prediction is where you say what will happen.

eg The group's prediction that the turtle would reach the end of the screen was incorrect.

presentation (*pre-zen-tay-shun*)
noun

A presentation is an illustrated talk or explanation given to an audience.

eg Mr. Thomas gave an interesting presentation to the class on his recent visit to Uganda.

presentation software
noun

Presentation software is used to create slide shows, incorporating graphics and images. It is used a great deal at business meetings as well as in the classroom.

eg PowerPoint is one of the most popular kinds of presentation software.

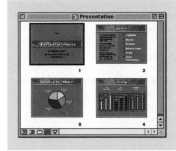

primary source
noun

A primary source is one written by the witnesses of an event, or one which directly quotes their words. Primary sources include letters, diaries, speeches and surveys which you have carried out yourself.

eg Martin Luther King's 'I have a dream' speech is an example of a primary source.

➡ **secondary source**

print
verb

To print is to transfer an electronic text or document to paper. 'Print' is a menu option in most software.

eg The class were told not to print off too many pages.

➡ **printer, print area**

print area
noun

The print area is a specified area of a document that is printed out.

eg If some of your document is not printed out then you will have to set the print area.

printer
noun

A printer is a peripheral connected to your computer that

A B C D E F G H I J K L M N O P Q R S T U V W X Y Z

allows you to transfer electronic documents to paper.

eg Inkjet and laser are both kinds of printer.

➡ **peripheral**

probe
noun

A probe is a device used for the purpose of monitoring or collecting data.

eg I used a temperature probe to record the temperature of the food whilst it was cooking.

procedure
noun

A procedure is a self-contained part of a program. It can be re-used whenever needed while the program is running.

eg Nicola wrote a procedure in Logo to draw a triangle.

process
noun

1 A process is the act of running a program on a particular occasion.

eg The processes running on my computer at the moment are the wordprocessor application and the operating system.

2 Process is also used in a general sense to mean the stages leading to a result.

eg The spreadsheet put the data through a process in order to calculate everybody's wages.

produce
verb

To produce something is to make it or cause it to appear.

eg The class were told to produce evidence for their conclusions.

program
noun

A program is a set of instructions carried out by a computer in order to achieve a particular end. Sometimes a program is referred to as software.

eg He bought a virus detector program and installed it on his computer.

➡ **software**

projection (*pro-jec-shun*)
noun

The image shown on the large screen or whiteboard when you use a projector is the projection.

eg With a projector and laptop you can show your PowerPoint presentation in any classroom.

➡ **projector**

project management
noun

Project management is coordination of all the resources needed to solve a problem. This is so that the work is completed on time and as efficiently as possible.

The congestion charge software was finished in time and worked well on its first day because the project management had been very effective.

projector ✉
noun

A projector is a piece of equipment, connected to a computer, which transmits an image from a computer screen to a large screen, whiteboard or wall.

The teacher used a projector to show the painting on the large screen so that the class could examine it in more detail.

➡ projection

protocol ✉
noun

A protocol is a set of rules controlling the way in which two computer systems can exchange data with each other. (Protocols also apply to other communication devices such as telephones.)

There are many different computer protocols in use, controlling everything from the school network to the Internet.

pseudo random number
(*su-do*)
noun

The word 'pseudo' means false or untrue. So a pseudo random number is a number that appears to be random but is not really.

A pseudo random number generator is a program used in probability and statistics when large quantities of random digits are needed. A pseudo random number generator does not generate truly random numbers. It has a finite number of states and the sequence of numbers It generates will eventually start to repeat itself.

public information system ✉
noun

A public information system is any organised way, computerised or otherwise, of distributing information which is intended to be useful for all people in a community. Such systems are usually set up by governments or other national organisations.

The National Grid for Learning (NGfL) is a UK public information system that links education, library and museum services.

purpose
noun

The purpose is the aim of something.

Before you design a website you should first consider its purpose.

ABCDEFGHIJKLMNOP QRST UVWXYZ

qualitative data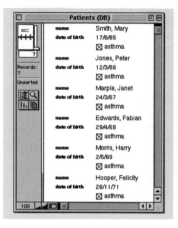
noun

Qualitative data is a type of information that is concerned with descriptions and opinions rather than quantities or numbers. It includes transcripts of interviews or focus groups.

🔍 The group decided they needed some qualitative data for their project. They went to the youth club and interviewed some teenagers about their opinions on activities for young people. The notes of the interviews were qualitative data.

➡ quantitative data

quantitative data
noun

Quantitative data is concerned with number or quantities.

🔍 The market research company sent out some questionnaires. The significant quantitative data they found was that 70% of people were satisfied with their present brand of washing powder, and that 45% did not use a fabric conditioner.

➡ qualitative data

query (*kweer-ee*)
noun

A query is a search of a database for a certain collection of records.

🔍 Nurse Powell wanted to find all patients suffering from asthma who were between 30 and 40 years of age, so this was her database query.

Patients (DB)		
name	Smith, Mary	
date of birth	17/6/65	☒ asthma
name	Jones, Peter	
date of birth	12/3/66	☒ asthma
name	Marple, Janet	
date of birth	24/3/67	☒ asthma
name	Edwards, Fabian	
date of birth	29/4/68	☒ asthma
name	Morris, Harry	
date of birth	2/5/69	☒ asthma
name	Hooper, Felicity	
date of birth	26/11/71	☒ asthma

questionnaire
noun

A questionnaire is a set of written questions given to people. The results are a set of statistics which can be analysed.

🔍 Frank sent the questionnaire by post to the people he wanted to answer it.

6. Do you buy *Yummo* dogfood?

| always | often | sometimes ✔ | rarely | never |

7. Do you watch *Channel 7* on TV?

| always | often ✔ | sometimes | rarely | never |

8. How many watches do you own?

| 8 or more | 4 to 7 | 2 or 3 | 1 ✔ | none |

9. Who is your favourite actress?

Cate Blanchett

random access memory [RAM]

noun

Random access memory (RAM) is the main memory of a computer. It stores the programs that are running and any data that is being processed. It loses its data when the power is switched off.

eg Felicity's computer contains 256 MB of random access memory, so it should be able to run large programs.

168-pin 133MHz SIMMs		
Size	Speed	Order No.
64MB	8ns	AB168/64
128MB	8ns	AB168/128
256MB	8ns	AB168/256
168-pin 100MHz SIMMs		
Size	Speed	Order No

MEMORY UPGRADES

random number

noun

A random number is one which is chosen in a completely unpredictable way.

eg Nobody can predict the results of the lottery because the machine produces a set of random numbers.

random number generator

noun

A random number generator is a program which uses a mathematical formula to produce a sequence of numbers which is random i.e. it has no pattern.

eg I used a random number generator to come up with numerical test data for my spreadsheet.

range

noun

The range is the spread of data; it is the difference between the greatest and least values.

eg The top salary was £70,000 and the bottom salary was £20,000 so the range was £50,000.

raw data

noun

Raw data is data that has not been processed.

eg The number of people watching the football matches had not been organised into groups so it was still raw data.

readability

noun

Readability is an assessment of how easy something is to read. Some word-processing programs will measure the readability of what you have written.

eg If you are writing a story for a five-year-old then it is essential you consider the readability of what you have written.

Readability Statistics	
Counts	
Words	1861
Characters	9551
Paragraphs	61
Sentences	93
Averages	
Sentences per Paragraph	2.0
Words per Sentence	17.0
Characters per Word	5.0
Readability	
Passive Sentences	9%
Flesch Reading Ease	40.6
Flesch-Kincaid Grade Level	11.6

OK

A
B
C
D
E
F
G
H
I
J
K
L
M
N
O
P
Q

R

S
T
U
V
W
X
Y
Z

record
noun

A record is a collection of fields in a database. If the fields were 'animal', 'colour', 'name', then one record might be 'cat', 'black', 'Felix'.

eg In order to deal with the complaint, customer services accessed the record of the customer in the database.

```
┌──────── Customer Database (DB) ───────┐
│  firstname    Mary                     │
│  surname      McCorquindale            │
│  addr1        155 Durham Terrace       │
│  addr2        Cheffarn                 │
│  addr3        Cornwall                 │
│  postcode     TX15 1BB                 │
│  tel          01973 884476             │
│                                        │
│  firstname    John                     │
│  surname      Evans                    │
│  Page 1                                │
└────────────────────────────────────────┘
Records: 128   Selected: 1   Unsorted   80   100
```

➡ field

refine
verb

To refine is to improve something. A computer makes it very easy to refine your work so that it is as good as it can be.

eg Cleo continued to refine her project until it was grade A standard.

relationship
noun

The way in which one thing connects to another is a relationship. In computers, it means that data in one part of a database is linked to data in another part.

eg The customer number in the customer table is linked to the customer number in the orders table by a relationship.

relative cell referencing
noun

When a spreadsheet formula is entered into a cell, it often refers to another cell. If the formula is copied, it adjusts to its new location. This process is called relative cell referencing. Relative cell referencing is the default on most spreadsheets.

eg Here is an example of when you might use relative cell referencing.

The **Total with VAT** is calculated by adding the **Cost of ITEM** (2 columns to the left on the same row) to the **VAT** for the item (1 column to the left on the same row) so the formula uses *relative* addressing.

```
C6          =B6+A6
┌──────────── VAT Calculation ───────────┐
│        A            B           C       │
│ 1  A VAT Calculator                     │
│ 2                                       │
│ 3  Rate of VAT =   17.50%               │
│ 4                                       │
│ 5  Cost of ITEM     VAT    Total with VAT│
│ 6      £50.00      £8.75       £58.75    │
│ 7      £23.50      £4.11                 │
│ 8      £12.25      £2.14                 │
│ 9      £12.40      £2.17                 │
│ 10                                      │
│ Sheet1 / Sheet2 / Sheet3                │
│ Ready                                   │
└────────────────────────────────────────┘
```

As the formula is copied down the column the formula changes and always refers to cells which are 2 columns to the left plus 1 column to the left relative to the cell with the formula.

```
┌──────────── VAT Calculation ───────────┐
│        A            B           C       │
│ 1  A VAT Calculator                     │
│ 2                                       │
│ 3  Rate of VAT =   17.50%               │
│ 4                                       │
│ 5  Cost of ITEM     VAT    Total with VAT│
│ 6      £50.00      £8.75      =B6+A6     │
│ 7      £23.50      £4.11      =B7+A7     │
│ 8      £12.25      £2.14      =B8+A8     │
│ 9      £12.40      £2.17      =B9+A9     │
│ 10                                      │
│ Sheet1 / Sheet2 / Sheet3                │
│ Ready                                   │
└────────────────────────────────────────┘
```

➡ absolute cell referencing, formula

reliable
adjective

If something is reliable then you can trust that it is correct.

eg The website was judged to be a reliable source of information.

remote datalogging
noun

Remote datalogging is when the data collected in a datalogging session has to be transferred to a storage device or computer in a different location. It may be collected on a disk or transmitted by telephone or radio link.

eg The air temperatures in the Arctic were obtained by remote datalogging – the data was transmitted back to the laboratory by radio.

➡ **datalogging**

remote sensing
noun

Remote sensing is the process whereby a sensor collects data which is later transferred to a computer.

eg Remote sensing can be used to collect information on the weather.

➡ **remote datalogging**

repeat
verb

To repeat something is to do it again.

eg The pupils repeated the exercise after changing one of the instructions.

repeated process
noun

Repeated process is a term given to a series of computer instructions/operations/code that are repetitively performed bringing about a result.

eg The factory robots are able to run continuously because of a repeated process: the instructions restart the same procedure after it has finished.

replicate
verb

To replicate is to copy something or make it occur again.

eg In order to track down the error, the programmer tried to replicate the problem experienced by the user.

replication
noun

A replication is a copy of something. The word is often used in connection with databases when part of a database is copied from the server to a client's computer. The copy or replication can be searched offline and updated, saving on network traffic.

eg On the Internet a replication of a website is called a mirror site.

report
noun

A report is the printed results from searching a database.

eg The teacher explained they needed a report of their search for their portfolios.

represent
verb

To represent is to make something stand for something else.

eg The CD-ROM was designed to represent a rain forest.

➡ **representation, simulate**

representation
noun

A representation is a model that attempts to mimic a process or thing in the real world.

eg The wave software was a representation of the action and shape of real water waves.

➡ **represent, simulate**

representative
adjective

If something is representative then it stands for something else, giving a true account of it.

eg They interviewed 5000 people to find out how they would vote in the next election: this was a representative sample of public opinion.

rescale
verb

To rescale is to change the scale on an axis of a graph or chart.

eg I rescaled the vertical axis on the graph to show between 80°C and 100°C so I could look in more detail at what was happening between these points.

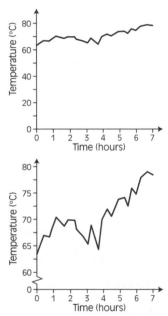

resize
verb

To resize is to change the size of a window or graphic by dragging on one of the handles with your mouse, or by using the 'resize' feature of a graphics manipulation program.

eg He decided to resize the image so that it made a greater impact on the page.

resolution (*re-so-loo-shun*)
noun

The resolution is the number of pixels displayed on your computer screen. It is generally written down as two numbers: the first gives the number of pixels that can be displayed horizontally on the screen; the second gives the vertical number of pixels.

eg She altered the resolution on her screen from 1024 × 768 to 1280 × 1024.

➡ pixel

review
verb

To review is to look over what you have done.

eg Before they began the second stage of the project they needed to review the first stage.
➡ revise

revise
verb

To revise is to look over what you have done and correct it.

eg He decided to completely revise his design after the comments from users.
➡ review

robot
noun

A robot is a computer-controlled machine capable of performing physical tasks.

eg Many of the manual jobs which used to be performed by people on production lines are now carried out by robots.

The word robot comes from *robota*, a Czech word meaning drudgery. The term robot was used in a Czech science fiction play by Karel Capek, written in the 1920s.

➡ repeated process

Roman
noun

Roman type is a style of serif font based on the letters of Ancient Rome. The letters are spaced proportionately and have serifs.

eg Times New Roman is a type of font, often used in newspapers because of its readability.

Times New Roman

ABCDEFGHI
JKLMNOPQ
RSTUVWXYZ
abcdefghijklm
nopqrstuvwxyz
1234567890
!@£$%^&*()

➡ serif

row
noun

The space between two horizontal lines on a spreadsheet or table is called a row.

eg You can easily add a row to a table.

	A	B	C
	Book Title	Height	Width
2	Gulliver's Travels	180	140
3	The Hobbit	170	120
4	Dictionary	230	165
5	Mountains	270	220
6	Jungle Animals	250	130
7	Mary's Game	210	150
8	Famous People	260	200
9	Oliver Twist	170	120
10	The Tudors	280	200
11	Life in France	280	200

➡ column, spreadsheet, table

rule
noun

A standard method or procedure for solving a problem is known as a rule.

eg The rule to convert between Celsius and Fahrenheit is multiply by 1.8 and add 32.

Ss

sample (*sam-pul*)
noun

A sample is a selection.

eg 1 When you carry out a survey you cannot interview everyone so you choose a sample of people.
2 In recording music electronically you can take a sample from an existing recording and incorporate it into another one.

➡ sample composition, sample size

sample composition
noun

A sample composition is the way in which a sample is made up, what it consists of.

eg Before carrying out the survey they looked at the sample composition. They made sure that males, females, different age ranges and income groups were all represented.

➡ sample, sample size

sample size
noun

Sample size is the number of people or things in your sample.

eg If you conduct a survey with a sample size of a thousand people, will your conclusions be valid for the UK as a whole?

➡ sample, sample composition,

sans serif (*sans ser-if*)
noun

A serif is a short decorative feature added at the end of a stroke to a letter. The word 'sans' is French for 'without', so a font that is sans serif does not have the serif feature. Arial is an example of a sans serif font.

eg In text aimed at young children it is best to use a sans serif font.

Arial

ABCDEFGHI
JKLMNOPQ
RSTUVWXYZ
abcdefghijk
lmnopqrstu
vwxyz
1234567890
!@£$%^&*()

➡ font, serif

satellite
noun

A satellite is a man-made device that orbits the earth. Satellites can be used to transmit voice, television, and data signals.

eg You can connect to the Internet by satellite.

save
verb

To save means to keep a file. Saving transfers data from random access memory to the storage medium – usually a disk. 'Save' is a menu option in most software packages.

🔵 The class was told to save their work so that they could continue with it next week.

scale
verb

To scale means to change the size of a graphic in a document.

🔵 She inserted a picture into the document and then decided to scale it for maximum impact.

➡ resize

scanner
noun

A scanner is a peripheral attached to your computer. You can copy an image or text printed on paper, and save it to your computer.

🔵 He used a scanner to copy the 1977 class photograph, and then sent it to the Friends Reunited website.

scatter graph
noun

A scatter graph compares two variables by plotting one value against the other.

🔵

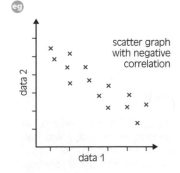

scatter graph with negative correlation

data 2

data 1

➡ line of best fit

schema (skee-ma)
noun

A schema is the organisation and structure of a database.

🔵 The schema for the database outlined the data type of the fields that made up each record.

➡ data type, file, record

screen
noun

The screen is another name for the monitor on your computer where information is displayed.

🔵 A screen can come in many different sizes – 15 inch and 17 inch are the most common for desktop computers.

A B C D E F G H I J K L M N O P Q R S T U V W X Y Z

A B C D E F G H I J K L M N O P Q R S T U V W X Y Z

scroll
verb

To scroll is to move the window display up and down or from side to side, viewing different information. You do this by dragging the horizontal or vertical scroll bar with a mouse.

eg He thought he had lost his work but the teacher told him to scroll down.

➡ scroll bar

scroll bar
noun

The scroll bar can be found on the vertical edge of a window and sometimes on the horizontal. You use it to adjust the text or graphics on display on the screen. The types of scroll bar vary with different operating systems.

eg When you are viewing a wide spreadsheet you certainly need a horizontal scroll bar.

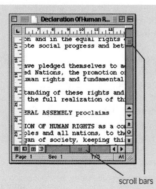

scroll bars

➡ scroll

search
verb

To search is to look for something. In computing it is often used to mean the action of looking for information on the Internet using a search engine.

eg She decided to search for information on Harry Potter using a search engine.

➡ search engine

search engine
noun

A search engine is a service provided on the Internet and is used to find web pages on a particular topic or area by entering key words or phrases. A program in the search engine called a spider or bot, identifies the pages containing these words and displays the findings as a series of hyperlinks.

eg Google is one of the most popular search engines.

search method/technique
noun

The search method or technique is the way in which you search for information on the Internet. The two main techniques are simple word searches and advanced or structured searches. On a simple word search the key word is entered in a box and the search engine identifies all pages containing those words. In an advanced or structured search, you can refine your search using Boolean connectors.

eg The simple search brought up too many pages, so he narrowed it down by using the advanced search.
➡ **Boolean connector, search, search engine**

secondary source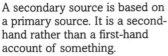
noun

A secondary source is based on a primary source. It is a second-hand rather than a first-hand account of something.

eg A biography of Princess Diana is a secondary source.
➡ **primary source**

sensor
noun

A sensor is an electronic device that can measure changes in the environment, e.g. heat, light or pressure.

eg The sensor measured the rate at which tea cooled in a glass cup.

➡ **datalogging**

sequence
noun

A sequence is a series of things in a certain order.

eg Joshua arranged his Powerpoint slides into a sequence which matched the points of his speech.
➡ **sequence of instructions**

sequence of instructions
noun

A sequence of instructions is important in control work. You have to decide what you want to achieve, write instructions and then put them in the best sequence or order.

eg If you want to control a small robot then you have to develop a sequence of instructions.
➡ **control, sequence**

serif (*ser-if*)
noun

A serif is a short decorative feature added at the end of a stroke to a letter. Bookman is an example of a serif font.

eg A serif font is often chosen for important, official documents that are printed out.

Bookman

ABCDEFG
HIJKLMN
OPQRSTU
VWXYZ
abcdefghij
klmnopqrs
tuvwxyz
1234567890
!@£$%^&*()

server
noun

A server is a computer that provides files for a network of computers, either locally or on the Internet. As many work stations will request files it needs

to be powerful with a lot of memory.

🔲 The website was not accessible as the server wasn't working.

shared area   ✉

noun

The shared area is a part of a school network that can be accessed by staff and pupils.

🔲 The teacher told that the class that the document could be found in the shared area.

simulate   ✍

verb

To simulate is to take on the appearance of something.

🔲 The PC game Premiership Manager tries to simulate what it is like to mange a football club.

➡ simulation

simulation   ✍

noun

A simulation is an imitation of a process, usually on a computer system. It makes use of a model in order to seem as close to reality as possible.

🔲 By using a simulation, Helen was able to experience what is was like to fly a plane without actually leaving the ground.

slide show   ✉

noun

A slide show is a presentation of a series of slides with images and text.

🔲 Cathy created a slide show to present her geography project to the class.

➡ slide view

slide view   ✉

noun

Slide view is an option in presentation software such as PowerPoint. It allows you to view an individual slide and alter the contents.

🔲 In slide view, the slides are displayed one at a time which makes it easier for you to add text, graphics, shapes, animations and multimedia.

➡ slide show

software   🔍

noun

Software is the name given to the programs that run on a computer. Software consists of instructions which tell the computer what to do. An operating system is the software that controls the hardware. Applications software performs the useful jobs that people want the computer to do such as working out people's pay.

🔲 Kirsty used desktop publishing software to lay out the pages of the newsletter.

➡ hardware, software

sort
verb

To sort is to arrange a series of items in a database in a particular order. For example, the order can be chronological, numerical or alphabetical.

🅴 The librarian decided to sort the book stock alphabetically on the database.

➡ **database, field, record**

sound
noun

Sound is a feature of a multimedia computer. Sound can be recorded, played and stored in sound files.

🅴 You can add sound to key moments in your PowerPoint presentations.

➡ **MP3, speakers**

speakers
noun

Speakers on your computer enable you to play and hear sound. They can either be separate devices, like those shown below, or built in to the computer.

🅴 He couldn't hear the sound of the music, so he checked to see if he had switched on the speakers.

spell-check
noun

A spell-check is a feature of word-processing software. It allows you to check your spelling. If you use spell-check on your work you will almost certainly receive higher marks for it, so it is a habit worth cultivating.

🅴 Some kinds of spell-check automatically underline spelling errors.

spreadsheet
noun

A spreadsheet application is a computer program that allows you to electronically create and manipulate spreadsheets. In an individual spreadsheet you enter each value in a cell. The spreadsheet allows you to define what type of data is in each cell such as numeric data or text. You can also define how different cells depend on one another. These relationships between cells are called formulae. With a spreadsheet you can carry out a 'what if' analysis by changing a value and seeing the effect on other values. You can also produce charts and graphs from the data in a spreadsheet.

state table – storyboard

A B C D E F G H I J K L M N O P Q R S T U V W X Y Z

(eg) Tony changed the value for the price of the product in the spreadsheet to see how much profit the company would make next year.

	A	B	C
	Prnfit Calculation		
1	**Annual Profit Forecast**		
2			
3	Number sold	1500.00	
4	**Price each**	£2.55	
5	Total Sales		£3,825.00
6			
7	Cost per item	£1.11	
8	**Total cost**		£1,665.00
9			
10	Other costs		£1,100.00
11			
12	Profit		£1,060.00
13			
14			

Sheet1 / Sheet2 / Sheet3
Ready

[i] The spreadsheet was introduced in business in the 1980s, and became popular because it could carry out calculations at speed. An early spreadsheet application was called VISICALC.
➡ **cell, formula**

state table
noun

A state table is used to specify the modules, input, outputs and actions for each part of a control system.

(eg) Here is an example state table for a control system where a single car enters a barrier controlled, fee-paying car park:

Car Park Barrier State Table

	Light beam detecting car	Traffic light at barrier	Barrier	Ticket dispensed
Car approaches barrier	on	Red	Down	No
Car stops at barrier	off	Red	Down	Yes
Driver takes ticket	off	Red	Up	No
Car passes under barrier	on	Green	Up	No
Car drives into parking area	on	Red	Down	No

(eg) Tom planned his control system and then drew up a state table to check how it might work in detail.

still image
noun

A still image is an image that does not move.

(eg) A still image was added to the web page.
➡ **moving image**

storage (*staw-ridge*)
noun

Storage is the collective name for any device for storing data such as CD-RW, floppy disk drive or hard drive. It can be internal, inside your computer, or external, another device connected by cable.

(eg) These days, the computer user has many different choices of storage. For those who make their own videos than an external, hard drive, with the ability to hold a large amount of data, has become increasingly popular.
➡ **CD-RW, floppy drive, hard disk drive, zip drive**

store
verb

To store is to keep a copy of data which you may retrieve or use later.

(eg) The web page looked interesting so he decided to store a copy.
➡ **save**

storyboard
noun

A storyboard is the outline plot of a film, presented as a series of sketches.

(eg) Before they used the video camera to film their play, they decided it would be best to plan it out with a storyboard.

➡ **storyboarding**

storyboarding
noun

Storyboarding is the process of creating a storyboard – the outline plot of a film, presented as a series of sketches.

eg Storyboarding is a skill you need to develop when creating moving images.

structure
noun

The structure of something is the way it is made up of different parts.

eg A database structure is made up of records and fields.

style
noun

The style of a document is how it looks on the page. The style includes font, font size, spacing, justification and so on.

eg Many organisations have a house style and all printed documents have to conform to this.

➡ **style sheet, style template**

style sheet
noun

A style sheet is a guide to how a document should appear on the page, either online or in print. It includes conventions for font, font size, spacing, justification, logos etc. The style sheet can be built into the document so that the text automatically conforms to the conventions.

eg Many organisations have a style sheet and all printed documents and online pages have to conform to this.

➡ **style, style template**

style template
noun

A style template is used when creating documents such as web pages. The background, font, position of images and hyperlinks are already specified, and the text that is entered is displayed in that format.

eg A style template is a quick way of creating a web page.

subheading
noun

A subheading comes after the main heading in a document. It is a way of organising the material.

eg The main heading was 'Roger Lyle's Home Page' and the subheading was 'Hobbies.'

subtask
noun

A subtask is a key element which, alongside other subtasks, forms a main task. The 'main' task is an umbrella term for a series of smaller actions.

eg If the task is 'Get ready to go out' the subtasks are: have a shower, clean teeth, get dressed, style hair, apply toiletries, put on shoes and coat and find phone/wallet/keys. All of these terms constitute the task 'Getting ready to go out'.

surf
verb

To surf is to browse the web, not looking for any page in particular but seeing what turns up.

eg He liked to surf the web just to see what he could find.

survey
noun

A survey is a collection of data obtained by asking questions or looking at certain things.

eg They had to carry out a survey on existing skateboarding websites.

A B C D E F G H I J K L M N O P Q R S T U V W X Y Z

switch
noun

A switch is mechanical or electrical device for opening and closing a circuit with positions of either on or off.

eg He couldn't find the switch on the kettle.

synthesise (*sin-the-size*)
verb

1 To synthesise is to bring together separate elements or things.

eg In music recording you use a synthesiser to synthesise different sounds.

2 To synthesise is to combine various factors so as to form a new, complex product/scenario.

eg The variables in the model were used to synthesise possible outcomes for profit from the concert.

system
noun

A system is a set of connected components that interact with each other.

eg A computer system consists of hardware components that have been carefully chosen so that they work together and software programs that can run in the computer.

system design
noun

A system design is a detailed plan of the components of a computer program. It includes details of the files to be used, how the files are organised, the inputs and the outputs, the program modules to be written and how the screens will be laid out.

eg The new computer system was planned in detail by the analyst and the system design was then handed to the programming team for them to implement.

system life cycle
noun

The system life cycle is a planning system for managing information technology projects. It has the following stages:
1. Initiation or description of problem.
2. Task analysis and requirements definition.
3. Design of solution.
4. Installation/implementation.
5. Testing.
6. Evaluation.
7. Maintenance.

eg When the company decided to install the new software they were at the installation/implementation phase of the system life cycle.

table
noun

A table is an organised way of storing data, in rows and columns. Tables can be set up in spreadsheets or in word-processed documents. The word has a special meaning in databases, where a table is the basic unit of storage. Each table is set up to store details of one thing or entity.

eg The names and addresses of the pupils were stored in the database in the pupil table.

➡ relationship

tag
verb ✉

To tag is to classify content on the Internet using meta-tags. The content is given tags, such as 'author', 'date of creation', 'subject matter', and so on. If the content is given the correct tags then users will be able to easily find the information they need.

eg Neil decided to tag the document with 'John Steinbeck', 'American Literature', 'Biography'.

❓ A person who tags content on the Internet is called a 'tagger. The work they do is called 'tagging'.
➡ content, metadata, meta-tags, XML, tag

tags
noun (singular: tag) ✉

In HTML or other mark-up languages tags are used to indicate how some aspect of it, such as font size, should appear in the browser. Each tag appears in angled brackets to distinguish it from the other text e.g. <title>. These are referred to as HTML tags. A meta-tag is a key word that describes the content of a site.

eg People who write regularly in HTML get to know the tags for different effects. These are the meta tag key words for a BBC site:
<meta name='keywords'content= 'BBC, News, BBC News, news online, world, uk, international, foreign, british, online, service'>

❓ The earliest HTML document containing tags on the Internet dates from 13th November 1990. Tim Berners-Lee, the founder of the World Wide Web, had started to develop HTML two months earlier.
➡ hypertext mark-up language (HTML), meta-tags

tally
verb 🔍

To tally is to count by making marks.

eg They kept a tally of the colour of cars going past the school gates.

colour	tally	frequency
red	⊦⊦⊦⊦ ⊦⊦⊦⊦ II	12
blue	⊦⊦⊦⊦ II	7
white	III	3
black	⊦⊦⊦⊦ II	7

A
B
C
D
E
F
G
H
I
J
K
L
M
N
O
P
Q
R
S
T
U
V
W
X
Y
Z

tapes

noun (singular: tape)

Tapes are magnetically-coated strips of plastic used for storing data. One of the advantages is that they can hold large amounts of data – up to several gigabytes. As they are slow to access, tapes are really only used to back up the data on the server or for long-term storage.

eg The network manager restored the missing data using the backup data on tapes.

➡ **storage**

teleconferencing

noun

Teleconferencing is the process of holding a live discussion between people at different locations using speakers and dial-up phone lines. When a video camera is used and the participants can see each other – either still or moving images – this is called videoconferencing.

eg Teleconferencing is a cost-effective way of bringing people together for a briefing.

teletext

noun

Teletext is a textual information service produced by television companies and viewed on televisions with a teletext decoder.

eg Looking for cheap holidays is a popular use of teletext.

television [TV]

noun

A television is a device which receives signals which are then converted into pictures and sound. Until the arrival of digital television the signals were analogue. This means that the transmitted sound and pictures

were converted into electrical signals, and then converted back into sound and pictures by the television set. With digital transmission the sound and pictures are electronically converted into a digital signal, transmitted as a bit stream and then converted to sound and pictures by a digital television or decoder in the home.

eg You can now attach a keyboard to your television and receive and send e-mails.

Digital television gives a better picture than the conventional analogue signal, because buildings and power lines do not interfere with the signals. At present there is digital terrestrial television and digital television from satellite and cable. The digital terrestrial television signal is sent by local transmitters. Cable is mainly only available in cities, while 98% of UK homes can receive satellite signals. At some point between 2006 and 2010 the UK government has decided that all analogue transmitters will switch to digital. However, you will still be able to use your analogue TV by buying a digital decoder.

template
noun

A template is a master document specifying a certain layout to which content can be added.

eg Microsoft Office has lots of templates for letters, web pages and memos.

test
verb

To test is to try out something to see if it works.

eg Test your designs by conducting a series of timed races.

text
noun

Text is a type of data recognisable as words.

eg She edited the text before handing in her essay.

transfer
verb

To transfer something is to move it from one place to another.

eg She decided to transfer the data from one spreadsheet to another.

transmission speed
noun

Transmission speed is how fast data is sent. It is measured as a certain amount of data in a certain amount of time, for example, kilobytes per second.

eg The MP3 player boasts transmission speed of 280Kbps.

➡ **band width**

truncated scale
noun

A truncated scale is a scale on a graph or chart where part of the scale is left out, for example, it does not start at zero.

eg I used truncated scales on my scatter graph of height against arm span because there were no measurements below 140 cm.

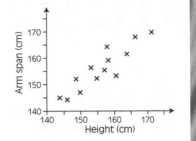

two-way table
noun

A two-way table is a summary of data divided up into two sets of categories. It shows how many individuals fall into particular combinations of categories.

eg My two-way table shows the number of students in my class who are either left or right-handed and also divides them into male and female.

	left	right	total
male	1	13	14
female	2	15	17
total	3	28	31

typeface
noun

The typeface is the design of individual characters. It usually means the same thing as font.

eg A good bold typeface was the best way of grabbing the readers' attention.

The complete Helvetica typeface

!"#$%&'()*+,./0123456
789:;<=>?@ABCDEFG
HIJKLMNOPQRSTUV
WXYZ[\]^_`abcdefghijk
lmnopqrstuvwxyz{|}~Ä
ÅÇÉÑÖÜáàâäãåçéèêë
íìîïñóòôöõúùûü†°¢£§•¶
ß®©™´¨≠ÆØ∞±≤≥¥µ∂
∑∏π∫ªºΩæø¿¡¬√ƒ≈∆«»
…ÃÕŒœ——""''÷◊ÿŸ/
¤‹›fifl‡·‚„‰ÂÊÁËÈÍÎÏÌÓ
Ôﬀ ÒÚÛÙı ˆ˜¯˘˙˚ ¸˝˛ˇ

➡ **font**

A
B
C
D
E
F
G
H
I
J
K
L
M
N
O
P
Q
R
S
T
U
V
W
X
Y
Z

underline
verb

To underline is to add a line underneath selected text. It is an option in word-processing software.

🔵 You can underline the bits of text you want to stand out.

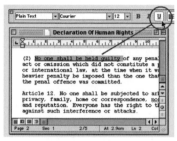

uniform resource locator [URL]
noun

A Uniform Resource Locator (URL) is the address of a file available on the Internet. The file can be, for example, a HTML page, a Java Applet or an image. The URL consists of a protocol, a domain name and the file location on the server.

🔵 Look at this URL: http://www.letts. co.uk/2003/aboutus.html

The protocol is http. This stands for HyperText Transfer Protocol and defines how the messages are transmitted and formatted.
The domain name is www.letts.co.uk and this is the server where the resource is located. The domain name has a suffix co.uk and from this we can tell that it is a UK website.
The file location is 2003/aboutus.html
The .html is the format of the file.

➡ domain name

universal product code [UPC]
noun

The Universal Product Code (UPC) was the first bar code to be widely adopted.

🔵 Bar codes were first put into use in 1973 by the grocery industry. These bar codes were soon standardised as the Universal Product Code (UPC).

➡ bar code, EAN

unreliable
adjective

If something is unreliable then you cannot trust it.

🔵 Some websites can be a source of unreliable information as you can publish virtually anything on the web.

upload
verb

To upload is to copy a file from a client computer to a server. The word usually refers to the copying of files to a web server.

🔵 Thursday was the day to upload new materials on the Anglia Campus website.

➡ download

upper case ✉

adjective

Letters are described as upper case if they are the capital letters of the alphabet.

eg Your table will be easier to read if you use an upper case letter to start each column heading.

ℹ On forums, e-mails and newsgroups, the use of upper case or capital letters in the text of a message signifies that you are shouting. So, unless you are shouting, it is best to just use capital letters for the traditional purposes.

➡ lower case

A
B
C
D
E
F
G
H
I
J
K
L
M
N
O
P
Q
R
S
T

U

V
W
X
Y
Z

validate

verb

To validate means for computer software to check that the data being input is sensible.

eg The applicant's age was validated to make sure that nobody over 65 or under 18 was entered into the database.
➡ **verification, verify**

validation
noun

Validation is the process of checking that the data being input is sensible. The word is always used to describe a computer process rather than a human process.

eg The bar code is put through a validation process to make sure that the correct number of bars is read.
➡ **verification**

value
noun

A value is the quantity or data item that is stored in a variable.
eg The value of pi is taken as 3.142

variable
noun

A variable is a location in memory, normally given a name, which stores data that can change.

eg The temperature reading was stored in a variable called Temp.

vector graphic
noun

A vector graphic, or vector image, is an image which is defined by a mathematical formula and not by individual pixels. For example the start and end points of a line are defined and the software constructs a line between them. Unlike bitmapped graphics, vector graphics do not degrade when they are enlarged.

eg The drawing package in the wordprocessor produces vector graphics which are easy to re-size without losing detail.

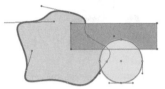

➡ **bitmap, pixel**

verification

noun

Verification is the process of checking that input data is correct. It is normally carried out by a human who visually compares the data with the source document.

eg In one good method of verification, the data is entered twice by two different people. The computer checks the two versions for differences. The differences are then checked visually by the data entry staff.
➡ **validation**

verify

verb

To verify is to check that the input data is correct. This is carried out by humans, sometimes with the help of the computer.

eg The data entry clerk verified that the names in the database matched those on the paper forms exactly.
➡ **validate**

video cassette recorder [VCR]
noun

A video cassette recorder (VCR) is linked to a television and is a means of playing and recording videos. The video images can be digitalised and stored on a computer for editing.

eg In a recent survey it was found that many parents have difficulty in setting a VCR and have to rely on their children to do it for them.

The first VCR was unveiled by Sony of Japan in 1975 and used a Betamax system. However, rival Japanese electronic companies introduced their own VCR system, called VHS. The two systems were completely incompatible. For a while the two formats ran alongside each other but Sony failed to market Betamax effectively and in 1988 they discontinued the product.

video clip
noun

A video clip is a small extract from a video often available on a website. You need software such as RealPlayer® or Quicktime® to view it.

eg If you want to play video clips on your computer then it is best to have a broadband connection.

➡ broadband

video conferencing
noun

Video conferencing is the process of holding a live discussion between people in different places, where they can see and hear each other. Cameras and specific software are required.

eg Some schools share a teacher and a lesson by using video conferencing.
➡ teleconferencing

video memory
noun

Video memory is an area of your computer's memory that is used for storing images before displaying them on the screen.

eg The amount of video memory on your computer affects the resolution and colour depth.

viewpoint
noun

The viewpoint is the perspective or point of view from which something is written.

eg The website contained accounts of evacuation during the war, written from the viewpoint of evacuees.
➡ primary source, secondary source

virus
noun

A virus is a small computer program, capable of copying itself and therefore transferring from one computer to another.

A B C D E F G H I J K L M N O P Q R S T U V W X Y Z

Some viruses are capable of destroying all the data on your computer, and sending themselves to all your contacts through your address book.

🔵 These days a virus is likely to be transmitted from an e-mail attachment or the Internet, so it is worth investing in some anti-virus software for your computer.

🔲 One of the most famous viruses was Bugbear in October 2002. Transmitted by e-mail, it crashed computers, distributed confidential e-mails and stole credit card details.

visitor
noun

A visitor is a person who uses a particular website.

🔵 Ann saw from the counter that she was not the only visitor to the site.

visitors since June

➡ **page impression**

voiceover
noun

A voiceover is recorded speech which can be added to a presentation. It is also referred to as a voice narration.

🔵 When preparing their PowerPoint presentation on 'David Copperfield' the pupils decided to present extracts from the book as a voiceover.

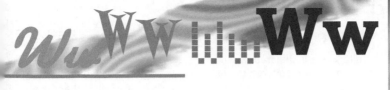

web browser
noun

A web browser is a software program that allows you to access and read web pages. The browser converts the HTML in which pages are written into readable text on your display screen.

(eg) Internet Explorer and Netscape Navigator are the most popular kinds of web browser, while Opera is another. All of them are free to download.

➡ hypertext mark-up language (HTML)

webcam
noun

A webcam is a low-cost video camera, often used on websites to provide online video footage.

(eg) Before he visited Barcelona he visited a website with a webcam, so that he could see what the city looked like.

web page
noun

A web page is a single page on a website, consisting of text and, usually, images. Pages are linked together by hyperlinks and written in HTML.

(eg) You can always add a new web page to your website.
➡ hypertext mark-up language (HTML), website

web publishing
noun

Web publishing is the process of writing and designing web pages, perhaps using a template or creating them from scratch in HTML, then putting them on the Internet, using an Internet service provider (ISP).

(eg) There are a range of templates available, such as those in Word, that make web publishing easier.
➡ hypertext mark-up language (HTML), Internet service provider (ISP), World Wide Web (WWW)

website
noun

A website is a collection of web pages on a server, which is part of the World Wide Web (WWW). The pages are written in HTML and are usually on a similar topic or theme. A website is accessed via its address or URL.

(eg) A website can have a variety of purposes: it can be used to sell things or it can just be a list of someone's hobbies or interests.

➡ hypertext mark-up language (HTML), uniform resource locator (URL), World Wide Web (WWW)

white space – wizard

white space
noun

White space is the area of a page that is not covered by text or graphics.

eg Large chunks of text crammed into a page make it look crowded: clever use of white space can make it easier to read.

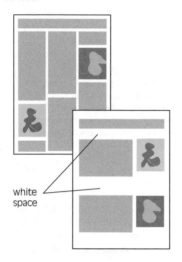

white space

wide area network [WAN]
noun

A wide area network (WAN) is a network where the computers are placed a distance apart, unlike a local area network where they are in the same or a nearby building.

eg The largest wide area network (WAN) in the world is the Internet.

➡ **local area network**

window
noun

A window is a rectangular display on your computer screen. You can scroll the contents of the window by using your mouse to move the cursor. You can operate several applications at once and open a window for each one; you can also open different files within an application and have a different window for each of them. You can resize a window by dragging on the corners with the mouse. You can also minimize a window, reducing it to an icon, or maximize it, so that it fills the whole screen.

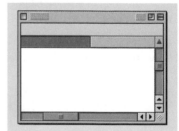

eg He opened a new window for his word processing application so that he could copy and paste some text into the website displayed in the browser.

i Both Macintosh and Microsoft operating systems allow you to work with different windows open. Microsoft named their operating system Windows because it has this capacity to work with different windows open.

wizard
noun

A wizard is a feature in software that helps the user to perform specific tasks. You are taken through a series of automated steps using the 'Next' button. You may be asked to choose from different options, enter text or tick a check box.

eg Greg used a letter wizard in his word-processing software to help him write a formal business letter.

i Microsoft's Windows 95 was the first operating system to use wizards.

wordprocessor
noun

A wordprocessor is software used to create and edit text. It usually has lots of other features to allow text to be displayed and laid out in various ways.

eg Karl used his wordprocessor to write a reference for Sarah.

World Wide Web [WWW]
noun

The World Wide Web (WWW) is the network of servers delivering web pages written in HTML to those with an Internet connection and a web browser. The World Wide Web allows users to access audio, graphics and video. The hypertext links in documents enable the user to jump form page to page.

eg Even if you don't own a computer you can still access the world wide web. Cyber cafes, libraries and multimedia payphones can all provide access, but of course you have to pay for this.

i The World Wide Web was opened in 1991 as a public service, although you have to pay for your Internet connection, and some web pages have subscription-only content. The web is largely uncensored and anyone can publish on it.

➡ **hypertext mark-up language (HTML), Internet, web browser, web publishing**

Xx

XML
noun

XML stands for EXtensible Mark-up Language. Like HTML, it is used for writing web pages that may be read by the user's browser. It is different to HTML in that it allows web developers to make up their own tags. This gives web developers the opportunity to include more metadata in a web page. Metadata is different kinds of information about the data.

eg XML will allow search engines to find the particular piece of information, for which a user is looking, more easily.

i XML was adopted as a standard in 1997 by W3C, the World Wide Web Consortium, a group of companies involved with developing a set of common standards for the Internet. It has been suggested by some people that XML will eventually replace HTML as the language in which web pages are written.

➡ **browse, hypertext mark-up language (HTML), metadata**

Y2K bug

noun

Y2K is another name for the year 2000. The Y2K bug was a concern about the ability of computer systems to cope with the turn of the century on 31/12/99 to 01/01/00. Some computer systems stored years as 2-digit numbers, and there was a possibility that the change in years could be seen as time going backwards. There were fears that planes could fall from the sky, supermarkets could run out of food and economic and social life could be completely disrupted.

eg The problems anticipated by the Y2K bug (the year 2000 bug) never actually happened because changes were made to computer systems well in advance of that date.

zip drive
noun

You use a zip disk in a zip drive, which can be either internal to your computer or external. It is a form of storage that can hold either 100 or 250 megabytes on a disk.

eg A zip drive is a useful way of backing up large files.

➡ zip file

zip file
noun

A zip file is a compressed file that can be sent more quickly over the Internet. Zip files are most useful when large files need to be sent or received. The software that zips and unzips the files is free.

eg Rather than sending the document through the post the publishers offered it as a zip file on their website.

➡ zip drive